Writing as a Road to Self-Discovery

by Barry Lane

About the Author

Barry Lane teaches that writing is a way to see new possibility in both personal lives and in the world at large. He teaches in prisons, public schools, colleges and literacy programs. He is coauthor with Bruce Ballenger of *Discovering the Writer Within* (Writer's Digest Books, 1989) and author of *After THE END: Teaching and Learning Creative Revision* (Heinemann, 1993). His essays and short stories have appeared in numerous magazines throughout the United States and his tape of original folk songs, *Lane's Recycled Fairy Tales* (New World Records, 1992) is a favorite among many teachers and children.

He currently lectures and conducts seminars on writing nationwide. He lives in Vermont.

WRITING

as a Road to

Self-Discovery

Barry Lane

WRITER'S DIGEST BOOKS
CINCINNATI, OHIO

Workshops
Barry Lane conducts seminars and writing retreats for educators, writers, businesspeople, literacy students, and anyone else interested in reclaiming their power as a writer.

For information call or write:
Discover Writing
P.O. Box 264
Shoreham, VT 05770
Phone or fax: (802)897-7022

Writing as a Road to Self-Discovery. Copyright © 1993 by Barry Lane. All rights reserved. No part of this book may be reproduced in any form or by any electronic or mechanical means including information storage and retrieval systems without permission in writing from the publisher, except by a reviewer, who may quote brief passages in a review. Published by Writer's Digest Books, an imprint of F&W Publications, Inc., 1507 Dana Avenue, Cincinnati, Ohio 45207. 1-800-289-0963. First edition.

Printed and bound in the United States of America.

97 96 95 94 93   5 4 3 2 1

Library of Congress Cataloging-in-Publication Data

Lane, Barry.
    Writing as a road to self-discovery / Barry Lane.
        p.   cm.
    Includes bibliographical references and index.
    ISBN 0-89879-537-0
    1. Authorship. I. Title.
PN151.L36   1993
808'.02—dc20

93-14535
CIP

Edited by Jack Heffron
Designed by Doris Eiber
Cover illustration by Clare Finney

For Carol-lee, now and forever
and
In loving memory of my father

Happy is the man whose strength
Thou art, O Lord,
Whose heart is a highway to Thee.
—Psalm 84

Acknowledgments

Thanks to my sister-in-law Leslie Goodrich, who single-handedly gutted the bathroom in the old part of our house and carried the toilet and clawfoot bathtub out into the yard to make a space for my office.

Thanks also to all my friends and ex-students, whose work appears within these pages and whose inspiration talked me into writing this book. I am grateful to my agent John White for help with research and to Ira Bruckner, Steven Worth, Alice Fogel, Andy Green, Verandah Porche and Richard Krawiec for ideas and inspiration.

Jack Heffron's editing skill, good humor and patience helped to nurture this project along, Bill Brohaugh's faith got it off the ground, and Terri Boemker's expertise made it look good. I am grateful.

On the psychological front, thanks to my brother Michael, and to my mother, for love and support during a difficult time. Thanks also to my uncle, Dr. Irwin Flescher, who has always been a role model for me as both a therapist and a writer, and to Robin Harris and Jim Hulfish, who showed me how to look and listen inside myself.

This book is dedicated to my wife, Carol-lee, whose steadfast support, love and eagle-eye editing constantly amaze me, and to the memory of my father, Leonard Lane, whose stories and love live on in his children and grandchildren.

Contents

Part Three: Reexperiencing

Techniques for tapping hidden powers of recollection and reflection in our writing and in our lives.

The Secret of Being Human

*My story is important not because it is mine . . . but because if I tell it anything
like right, the chances are you will recognize that in many ways it is yours.
Maybe nothing is more important than that we keep track . . . of these stories
of who we are and where we have come from and the people we have met
along the way because it is precisely through these stories in all their particular-
ity. . . that God makes himself known to each of us most powerfully and personally . . . . to lose track of our stories is to be profoundly impoverished not only
humanly but spiritually.*

*I not only have my secrets, I am my secrets. And you are yours. Our secrets
are human secrets, and our trusting each other enough to share them with each
other has much to do with the secret of what it means to be human.*

—Frederick Buechner

Words hold the keys to forgotten memories, feelings,
thoughts and new understandings. I've learned this from
the prisoners, school children, college freshmen, senior
citizens, homeless people and others who have attended my writing
classes. Whether it is a third-grader named Amy bringing to life
memories of her beloved grandmother or a prisoner named Mark
digging up painful childhood memories in order to understand the
lifetime of drug abuse and violence that landed him in jail, writing
is a way of rediscovering the past and building new understandings
for the present and future.

When we write from the heart, we return to the past and bring
with us all the knowledge we have gained since. Our life becomes a
novel or symphony and certain themes begin repeating themselves.

We can understand the events of our lives by reentering them with our current wisdom in our pockets. We can discover hidden secrets; heal painful memories; unleash joyful thoughts and visions; destroy outdated patterns of thought and behavior that cloud our thinking; create new ways of seeing ourselves, our families, our country and our world.

Writing is a form of verbal medicine. Used wisely, it can initiate self-discovery and healing.

The Three Questions

We can divide the self-discovery/healing process into three central questions:

1. What do I remember?
2. What do I know now that I didn't know then?
3. How does my newfound knowledge change me and the world around me?

The three sections of *Writing as a Road to Self-Discovery* reflect these three questions: remembering, reframing, reexperiencing. When we look at these three questions it's easy to see how the writing process mirrors the healing process.

Remembering is a powerful source of self-discovery and healing. Chapters 1–3 illustrate techniques to dig up old memories and to begin understanding the hidden meanings of the past.

Reframing (Chaps. 4–5) teaches different methods to reflect on your memories, make surprising connections, develop new ways of seeing, and discover a capacity for creative critical thinking you didn't know was inside you.

Once you know how to dig up memories and reflect about your world from different perspectives, you have gained a unique creative power that enables you to reexperience both the past and present world with new insight unclouded by unexamined patterns of thought.

Reexperiencing (Chaps. 6–8) illustrates ways to tap this power in your writing and your life. Exercises in this section focus on ways of gaining a new perspective on not only our personal lives, but also on the lives of the others sharing our planet. Writing can be a powerful tool for developing empathy, healing old wounds and reshaping our vision of the world we live in.

This Isn't Easy. Sometimes It Hurts! Why Should I Bother?

Language permits us to see. Without the word, we are all blind.
—*Carlos Fuentes*

We live in a world where old-world orders are crumbling and new ones are slowly emerging to maturity. Humanity is moving from its collective adolescence to a collective adulthood. While the vision of newly realized powers and capabilities, wisdom and grace seem almost within our eager, even desperate grasp, the turbulence of this time of transformation, from youth to adult, from potentiality to reality, is almost too frightening, too painful to endure. Indeed, to be trapped in this time of turbulence without a vision of who we are becoming, individually and collectively, is the most intolerable confusion and pain possible.

Now more than any time in history, imagination and self-reflection are survival skills of the highest priority. Intelligence researcher Howard Gardner has defined a quality known as *interpersonal intelligence*: The ability to imagine the other's point of view and respond out of that imaginative awareness. It is my hope that reading and using this book will help unchain your imagination so it can be put to use building a new world for yourself and your fellow earthlings. When we write from the heart we not only celebrate, we enhance our humanity.

How to Use This Book

Each chapter of *Writing as a Road to Self-Discovery* has several exercises and explanations, and ends with a series of triggers (a list of short exercises meant to trigger more memories, ideas or emotions). Though the chapters follow a loose sequence, I recommend using this book whichever way pleases you. You may leaf through to find chapters and exercises that grab your attention first. Think of these as jumping-off places for experiments. Don't feel compelled to try every exercise; rather, set aside some time to write each day (even ten minutes) and try the exercises that appeal to you. Don't lose your momentum or give in to the lethargy that often indicates you're getting close to the bone.

You can also read the book first and then go back and do the exercises from chapters that strike a nerve. You can read the book through and let it ferment on your shelf for months until your pen is ready to do the work. Or, you can sit down for an hour each day and work through each chapter.

If you choose to browse through this book, you will occasionally come across a term that was described in an earlier chapter. To make it easy for you, there is a complete glossary of all the writing techniques on pages 184-189.

But What if I'm Not a Writer?

If you are like most people, sitting down to write won't be easy at first. We all have voices that tell us we can't write. It's our job as writers to negotiate between the critical and creative voices in our heads.

Here's one idea: Write a letter to your self-critical side. The more you acknowledge your feelings about writing, the more you will allow your stories to emerge. Whenever you hear those voices of discouragement remember that this is part of the process; observe them, write them down, draw them, speak them. It's also helpful to record your positive writing experiences. Mapping your successes and failures will help you look back on your own unique process and find your way through difficult times.

Buy yourself some writing tools: a new pen, a nice blank journal, a notebook or a notebook computer. Treat yourself. You are going to write your heart out.

Forgiveness and Permission: Taking the Oath

Throughout *Writing as a Road to Self-Discovery* I have included samples of writers who have encountered what I call *core stories*, stories that connect with the central issues of a person's life. A goal of this book is to lead you to discover your own core story through your writing. When we connect with this material it helps us to accept and integrate forgotten experiences and memories into our lives.

Core stories are buried by layers of protective armor, in the form of denial, fear, anger, shame, sadness, etc. Before we can write with all our heart we must give ourselves permission to do so. A few months ago a young woman came up to me after a workshop and thanked me for giving her permission to write about a fearful childhood experience. "But I didn't give you permission," I said, a little surprised. She paused for a moment. "I guess I gave myself permission," she laughed.

Since then, whenever I do a workshop with any group from first grade on up, I ask people to give themselves permission to write down *all* that is inside them. This may seem a little silly at first, but I think you'll understand the importance and find yourself remembering this oath the more you write about the deep-down things.

So raise your right hand and repeat after me.

I, _____ _____, do hereby swear on this day of _____, to give myself permission to write down everything that is in my heart, my brain, my soul, my pen and every other part of my self.

Permission granted!

In some cases this oath of permission may not be enough. It's hard to grant yourself permission to write about things you still feel guilty about. Hence, here is one more oath.

I, _____ _____, on this day of _____, do hereby take compassion on myself for everything I have ever done or not done, thought or not thought, dreamed or not dreamed. I will counter shame with forgiveness, and allow my inner heart to share anything with me in our writings, dreams, drawings, etc.

Permission granted!

Believe in Yourself

Now that you have officially given yourself permission and forgiveness you are ready to remember, reframe and reexperience your world. All you need now is a pen or pencil and a sheet of paper the size of Wisconsin.

There is an old Hindu saying, "When you were born you cried and the world rejoiced. Live your life so that when you die you will rejoice and the world will cry." This book exists to help you discover all the unexpressed grief, joy, sadness, confusion, anger and awe inside you so that when you come to the end of this world's journey you will see the great light at the end of the tunnel, instead of just the dark secrets growing like moss along the sides.

Believe in yourself and write with all your heart and soul.

Part One

Remembering

. . . For the writer there is no oblivion. Only endless memory.
—Anita Brookner

• Chapter 1 •

Childhood: The Myth and the Reality

Memory believes before knowing remembers.
—William Faulkner

Your pen has a brain in it. It will remember and create things if you give it a chance. Writing is not dictation from brain to paper. Something miraculous happens when you write. A thought appears on the page that the writer didn't expect to see; an idea connects with another idea and suddenly the larger purpose of the writing shifts. Writing is a way of discovering truth in memory, and with that discovery comes new knowledge and insight.

If you are like me this might seem odd at first. I was taught that writing was simply a means to communicate, not a way to think or discover. My well-meaning school teachers undermined my creativity by assigning topics to write about instead of teaching me how to trust in my own imagination and interests. This book will teach you writing techniques to lead you to your best material. Don't be discouraged if you don't find it right away. Give yourself permission to experiment. Relax. In this chapter we begin our journey of discovery by remembering our childhoods through writing. Here's an exercise to begin the journey back in time.

Reentering a Memory

1. Find an old photograph of yourself as a child.

2. Describe the photograph as if you are a magic camera that can record physical sensations along with what you see. I call this concept a *snapshot* because the writer records only what he perceives through his senses. Confine your snapshot to physical detail like the snapshot of my father and me when I was four years old.

The man wears a suit with baggy pants. His hand is

on the boy's shoulder. The young boy wears a tweed overcoat, sunglasses and a fedora hat. His hands are in his pockets, his head turned to one side. The man holds a cigar in his left hand.

3. Ask yourself three questions to help you get more physical detail into your snapshot. For example:

What is the expression on the man's face?

Where are the boy's hands?

What is the background?

The man's mouth was open as his face was half in shadow. The boy's hands were stuffed into the pockets of his overcoat.

4. Next, imagine you are the same age as you were in the photograph. Take a *thoughtshot* of yourself back then. A thoughtshot is like a snapshot but focused on thoughts rather than sense perceptions. For example:

I don't want my picture taken. They are always taking my picture. Why do I always have to pretend I am someone else?

5. Now write a thoughtshot of yourself today looking at the photograph. Begin with a list of questions about either the first snapshot, the thoughtshot or the photograph itself. Answer the most compelling one and keep writing for ten minutes. For example:

Why did my parents always dress me like a gangster?

What is this sadness in me today? Is it grief for my deceased father or is it grief for something else?

What is it about cigars that made my father seem so self-confident?

My father knew how to hold a cigar, wedged in his

fingers, away from the body so the wind would take the dead ash and carry it away. And when he puffed it his face looked determined, hopeful and confident. I love the way my father held a cigar, the way smoke coiled off the end, into the air, the way it hovered in the air after he left the room.

Digging Deeper

What tone do you notice in your childhood voice? How does it affect your feelings about the picture you wrote about? What do you see when you compare your child voice to your adult voice?

The Mountain and the Sea

All writing begins in the sea of experience. As children we see things vividly; we smell, feel, touch and taste the world. We have experiences that embed themselves in our hearts and minds. You dove into the sea when you entered the photo and wrote from yourself as a child.

Yet when we write, we climb the mountain of perception. We look down and see patterns in our experiences with our adult minds. We make connections and see disparities. You did that when you wrote questions and thoughtshots of your snapshots and the photograph. You looked for patterns in your life and the stories that grew out of them. Powerful writing moves up and down the mountain, oftentimes in the same sentence.

In my travels as a writing teacher, I have seen many writers begin the climb up the mountain with little instruction from me. In most cases, simply providing a safe place to write and giving writers permission to explore their past experience is enough to begin the process of self-reflection and reparenting.

Ray began to climb the mountain of perception the moment he sat down to write about his deceased father.

Ray's Story

Ray was a barroom brawler in jail for assaulting a police officer. He was a short man with a scruffy beard who was considered a troublemaker by guards and a ring leader to inmates. On the first day of my writing class at the state prison he began to write about his father. His first pieces were sketchy. His father had died of cancer ten years earlier at the age of fifty. He loved his father and was shocked to have lost him. He wrote first about the funeral and the intense feelings of loyalty he shared with his sisters. He also lamented his father's death and that he never really got to know the old man.

I asked Ray to simply write more memories of his father as if his pen were a camera that could paint snapshots. In each snapshot his father appeared as a remote individual who was rarely home and related to his children only as an authoritarian presence. In his short piece, "The Asskicking," Ray described an unpleasant memory of his father.

The Asskicking

"Did you hear me?" the powerful man said.

"Yes, Dad."

"Why did you siphon gas from the neighbors?"

"I don't know. I guess I just wanted extra gas to cruise with."

"I'll give you something to siphon gas for."

With my feet barely touching the floor I saw my world go crashing. I caught a real quick glimpse of the powerful hand come towards me like a freight train about to collide with another.

My heart pounded. My body shook. I closed my eyes and wished I had never siphoned gas. I felt myself flying through the air with blurred pain in my head. Different shapes and colors flashed through my eyes. Then everything went dark.

I awoke a short time later to see my Dad standing over me.

"No," I said, "No more. I promise I'll never siphon gas again."

The more Ray wrote about his father, the more the real man came into focus and the myth faded. However, Ray's image of his father and his love for the man did not diminish; rather, he began to understand the flaws in their relationship and began the process of grieving, not simply for a dead father, but for the other father he never had in life, but wanted.

This became evident one night when Ray couldn't sleep. He crawled out of bed and sat on the cold cement floor of his prison cell. He looked out the window at the moonlit clouds and heard his father's voice calling him. The voice, which seemed to rise up from inside himself, said, "Everything's OK. Live life to the fullest wherever you are." Ray cried as he wrote his father's words in his composition book. He sat on the floor of his cell until the dawn light came through the window.

You could speculate on whether the voice Ray heard was from his deceased father. Whatever your conclusion, Ray had found something out through his writing and remembering. He had looked beyond his initial mental image of his father to a deeper realization of who the man truly was and what his memory meant to him. Later that year Ray would write about the drunken binge that landed him in jail and the moment his five-year-old son turned to him and asked, "Daddy, why did you hurt Mommy?" He couldn't get his son's words out of his mind and when he wrote them he wept once again because he knew he had abandoned his boy the way his father had abandoned him.

Psychologist Pia Melody describes a dysfunctional family as a place where the child's reality is ignored and ridiculed. Parents in such a family blame their children for less-than-perfect behaviors, which in a healthy family are tolerated and understood. Children from dysfunctional families learn to lie to themselves and hide their need to be parented. Then, later in life, they seek to fulfill these needs with another adult. For Ray, writing was a way to locate the truth about his childhood and begin reparenting himself.

I began writing this book in September 1991, two weeks after my second daughter was born. That very same week, my father died suddenly of a heart attack in his sleep. Like Ray, I was immediately struck by how much I loved my father and how much I missed him. I felt his love wash over me like a beautiful wave as I sat dumbstruck on the edge of the bathtub at 3:30 that morning. And though I knew my father was not a perfect person, his inadequacies and problems seemed so insignificant compared to his love for me and my love for him. At the time, I had no desire to write about my father and what he meant to me. The wound was too fresh, and I clutched his sacred memory to my chest like a warm pillow. But lately I find myself dreaming, scribbling and talking about my father constantly. It's almost as if his spirit is alive and it's telling me to take a look, to understand!

But where do I start? How do I learn to use writing as a tool for remembering my father? What will my words tell me of the other father inside me that Ray discovered in his writing?

Here are a few triggers that may get you remembering your first family.

Triggers

- Draw a cartoon picture of your family. Make each member a character. Don't worry about your artistic talent. Draw stick figures if you want. Have fun.

- Pretend you are another member of your family. Describe yourself from that person's point of view.

- Write a list of moments involving members of your childhood family. Pick one and freewrite about it.

- Continue freewriting for ten minutes from one of these prompts.

> "My family was . . ."
> "My father always . . ."
> "My mother always . . ."
> "My brother always . . ."
> "My sister always . . ."

- Create a family portrait of your family with words. You can invent a portrait or use a real photograph to go by.

- Write a quick sketch of a happy family. Now compare that family to your own.

- Write a short, "How to" poem about someone in your family. This one, by Catherine Lamb, was written in a humor workshop. We laughed when she read it to our group. But when she read it to the larger group everyone was still.

How to Be My Father
> Don't speak.
> Get a big chair.
> Sit in it six to eight hours at a time,
>> unless it's a weekend, then twelve to fourteen.

Read four newspapers a day.
Snore.
Yell at the TV.
Eat Donuts.
Smoke.
Say, "son of a bitch."
Don't go to do anything unless you get yelled at first,
    then say "son of a bitch."
Leave your boots in the living room.
Eat in front of the TV.
Complain about opening Christmas presents.
Say "Jesus Christ" when someone asks you to do some-
    thing.
Buy Christmas presents at the hardware store.
Break your chair by sitting in it too long.
Say "Jesus Christ,"
    or "God Damn it."
Go back to not speaking.

Tools for Remembering

How can I know what I think, till I see what I say?
                                              —E.M. Forster

For years psychologists have used writing as a cognitive tool. Dr. William Pithers, who heads the world-renowned sex offenders program for Vermont Prisons, begins his therapy by having sex offenders write a detailed autobiography. Pithers knows that 95 percent of all sex offenders were abused as children, and writing down these painful memories can be the first step in remembering events that have been clouded by years of rationalization. In their book, *The Courage to Heal* (HarperCollins, 1988), Ellen Bass and Laura Davis tell rape and incest victims about the enigmatic qualities of memory. "There is no right or wrong way when it comes to remembering. You may have multiple memories. Or you may just have one. . . . When you begin to remember, you might have new images every day for weeks on end. Or you might experience your memories in clumps, three or four of them coming at a time."

In the next section of this chapter I present several prewriting techniques to help you begin finding memories you thought you had forgotten. Try them out and see which one works best for you.

Write Before You Think: Freewriting

Freewriting, one of the best techniques for digging up new memories, is also the simplest. Pick a block of time—say seven minutes. Sit down in a comfortable place. Begin writing about something and don't stop until the time is up. Don't screen out thoughts or erase words. Rather, try to write faster than you think. If you get stuck, write your thoughts and follow those thoughts wherever they lead you. Don't worry if you get stuck once in a while or cross out a word. Devise your own method of freewriting to fit your personality. Remember, the goal here is fluency of thought to paper. Let's try it out.

Close your eyes and imagine the thoughts in your head are like a large lake. A river runs from your shoulder, down your arm and empties at the end of your pen. Freewrite your thoughts for five minutes.

Here are a few prompts to find memories through freewriting.

- Freewrite about your earliest memories.
- Freewrite about your first crush.
- Freewrite about a disappointing day.
- Freewrite about a childhood fear.
- Freewrite about a confusing memory.
- Freewrite about a first encounter with death.
- Freewrite about a time you made your parents proud.
- Freewrite about a time you lost something.

When you've finished your freewrite, read it over and circle any areas that intrigue you. Pay particular attention to those phrases that surprised you when you wrote them.

Webbing Your Life

Webbing is a nonlinear form of idea gathering. Think of yourself as possessing the ability to take a helicopter ride above your subject. Webbing will help you to see all the directions you can pursue.

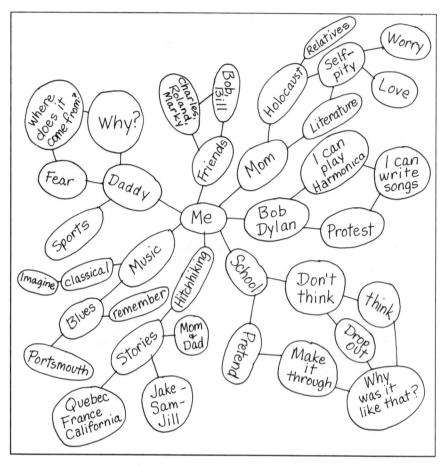

Try this:

• Put the word *Me* in the middle of a blank page and circle it. This is the nucleus of your web chart.

• Now try webbing all the people, things and events that have influenced your life. My web chart is shown above.

• Free associate ideas in separate strands off your nucleus.

• List influences. Relax and let the ideas pour from your pen. Return to the nucleus when one strand runs out.

• Let your chart grow intricate patterns and shapes. Use crayons and get a bigger piece of paper.

• Give yourself permission to embellish your chart with old photos or memories. Play with it for several days. Take time to marvel at a fresh memory. Write code words that will help you to remember without slowing you down.

• Stop and look at your chart. Circle areas that confuse, confound, puzzle or delight you. Start new charts on another page in your journal. Freewrite for seven minutes about one of the places you circled. Look for new ideas in your freewrite and web one of these discoveries.

Brainstorming Your Life

Brainstorming works for people who hate web charting.

To brainstorm ideas, simply list them down the page. Don't think about it too much and don't screen out ideas before they reach the page. You can also brainstorm a strand off your web chart. Here are the keys to a successful brainstorm.

• Don't screen things out. Bad lists often lead to good lists. See your thoughts as steps leading to each other.

• Write quickly.

• Don't worry about spelling, grammar or style.

Here's a brainstorm of things my father said and did and memories I have of him.

His scratchy beard.

Telling bedtime stories about growing up poor in New York City.

Playing football and baseball with him and my brother.

Him sitting in the car watching me play baseball—how good it felt that he was there.

Arguing about how to live.

Repairing the body of his old Chevy—Why was I so obsessed about it? He traded it in for a Cadillac.

As a child laying in bed waiting for him to come back from the races, waiting for the headlights to pour through the venetian blinds. That's when I first imagined his death. I knew he would die first.

Football cards under the pillow.

N.Y. Giants Y.A. Tittle; the Sunday football ritual.

Him taking us everywhere in the Ford Falcon.

His hand slamming against back seat to scare us into not making noise.

He never hit me.

If you want, try freewriting for seven minutes about one thing you circled on your list.

Snapshots

A *snapshot*, as you practiced at the beginning of this chapter, is simply a word picture of your subject that freezes time. As a writer, however, I have a great advantage over photographers because my descriptions can include sounds and smells as well as sights. The concept of the snapshot helps writers to focus their perceptions and dig deeper for details.

When we write a snapshot our first images are often blurry; as we ask ourselves questions, they grow sharper. Think of yourself holding up a pair of binoculars to your eyes. Each question you ask yourself helps to turn the knob on the binoculars to create a sharper image. Let me give you an example.

> My father driving the car.
> What's he doing? What kind of car? What color?
> My father gripping the bright red steering wheel of
> the 1965 Ford Falcon Futura.

As you write a snapshot, remember you are freezing one moment in time. Ask yourself questions and dig deeper for more details about that one moment. Delight as the word picture develops like a Polaroid with each new thought in front of you. Remember that as a writer you have a great advantage over most photographers because you can record smells and thoughts too.

Here are a few ideas for where to point your camera.
- Write a snapshot of your mother or father.
- Write a snapshot of a best friend.
- Write a snapshot of a secret place.
- Write a snapshot of an old car.
- Write a snapshot of a special moment.
- Write a snapshot of a frightening moment.

Thoughtshots

What I call a *thoughtshot* is simply a snapshot of a person's thoughts. We practiced this with the photograph at the beginning of this chapter. It could be your thoughts or the thoughts of a character or person you know. To write a thoughtshot, simply think about someone or something and write down your thoughts. Try writing a thoughtshot about one of the people or things on your web chart. Freewrite for seven minutes. Stop. Did any new thoughts emerge from your freewrite? Circle them. There may be a story there to develop in later chapters.

Cavewriting

Children have a remarkable capacity to depict their memories on paper. When given free rein to explore their imaginations, their lack of literary skills are not a problem because drawing and writing are not separate activities. I've seen kindergartners who can lecture for a half an hour about a few scribble marks on a piece of construction paper. The story is inside them; give them a crayon and a piece of paper and that story will get out.

As adults, unless we are deemed an artist, we are taught to disregard our drawing. We give it diminishing names like doodling and, at best, consider it a way of filling time. With the inspiration of children, I've developed a technique that reclaims our inner artist and gets raw memories and emotions down on a page. I call it cavewriting because it is the kind of writing I imagine cave people would do if they had an alphabet to mix with their painted images. I have always been awed by the raw primitive power of ancient cave paintings and have observed similar qualities in the writing of young children, who are as likely to draw a word as write it.

I did a cavewriting about the recent death of my father (shown on the next page). I drew a picture of his face in the coffin and I wrote down my emotions, my thoughts and my feelings at the moment I found out that he had died. There need not be any specific order to cavewriting. Some start with words. Some start with images. The point is to get the stuff on the paper. Try following this sequence and then experiment on your own.

1. Begin by picking a subject: a person, a place, a memory, a crazy idea, etc.

2. Scribble a picture of that subject. It doesn't have to be perfect or even remotely artistic. Give yourself permission to express that subject on the white page.

3. Write some single words or questions about your subject anywhere on the page.

4. Look at your cavewrite. Add more drawings or words. Hang it near your writing desk.

Try cavewriting about an unsettling moment in your life. Again, don't fret about your artistic ability. Let your words and the power of the emotion guide you. Be abstract if it pleases you. Above all, get it out there on the paper. Look at it and circle any parts that surprise or intrigue you. Keep this for future reference.

Body Mapping

Invite a friend over to make a *body map*. You need a magic marker and a person-size piece of paper (the kind you can sometimes get as endrolls at your local newspaper). Lie down on the paper and have a friend trace the outline of your body onto the paper. Look at the outline of your body and write memories from different parts of your body. Pick one or two intriguing memories and freewrite for twenty minutes on a blank piece of paper. Let your thoughts lead you to more memories of people, places and events associated with that part of your body.

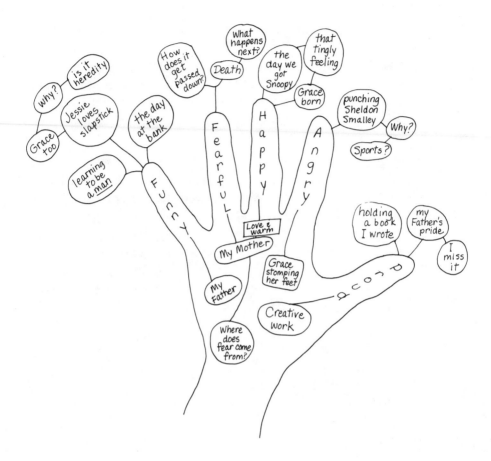

Hang your body map near your writing desk and add memories to it in idle moments.

Hand Mapping

A *hand map* is another way to involve your body in the quest to remember. Begin by tracing your hand onto a piece of blank paper (my hand map is shown above).

- Write a feeling or an aspect of your personality for each finger.
- Draw lines from each finger and write down experiences that connect with those feelings or aspects of your personality.

- Pick one intriguing event or feeling and freewrite for ten minutes.
- Find inventive ways to add to your map. For example, trace a child's hand onto the paper and write down a childhood need for each finger. Brainstorm memories triggered by those needs and freewrite about an intriguing one.

Chanting

A *chant* is a poem with a repeating line. Begin by brainstorming a list of phrases that have meaning to your life. They could be the familiar voice of a parent or child ("More juice, Mommy"), the voice of a feeling ("I'm so mad"), the voice of society ("Have a nice day").

- Pick one intriguing phrase from your list and put it at the top of a blank page in your journal. This is the chorus of your chant.
- Now write a poem where your chorus repeats, either every other line, or as often as you like. For example:

Lost at the A and P
I'm lost
   where am I?
I'm lost
   where are they?
I'm lost
   help me, Cheerios.
I'm lost
   save me, Fruit Loops.
I'm lost
   bring me home, Muzak.
I'm lost.

Digging Deeper

What intrigues you about your web chart, brainstorm, snapshot, thoughtshot, cavewrite, body map, hand map or chant? Which questions do you want to answer? Which ones shut you down? Which memory-gathering techniques work for you? Why?

Jane's Story

When the body is finally listened to it becomes eloquent. It's like changing a fiddle into a Stradivarius.

— Marian Woodman

I learned how writing feeds memory from Jane, a student in the first college freshman English class I taught. She was an older woman in her fifties and, like most returning students, felt a bit out of place with a room full of nineteen-year-olds. She had straight blonde hair and eyes that always seemed to be thinking and questioning. Her hand was the first to go up and her astute comments quickly helped me to realize I had an unpaid teacher's helper working for me.

Jane hadn't written since high school, where a teacher told her she wasn't creative. At a young age her father told her she was pretty so there was no need for her to go to college. Her younger sister went to Harvard and eventually received a doctoral degree; Jane married early and spent the next years as a homemaker.

Early on it was easy to see Jane was a gifted writer. She not only had a talent for remembering things in specific detail, she also had an instinct for what was important in her life. When I asked the class to brainstorm a list of earliest memories, Jane decided to write about a summer afternoon of berry picking in Mississippi where she grew up. But, as she wrote, she eventually learned why this memory clung to her mind when so many others had drifted away. As you read "Berry Picking" notice how Jane discovers the reality in a simple memory.

Berry Picking

It was a sixteen-acre berry patch crawling with snakes. It had, however, the most luscious dewberries imaginable. Fully ripe, dripping with juice and warm from the sun. They were hidden amongst thorns and brambles and lurking, always lurking beneath were huge black snakes. Sometimes they slithered away unseen, but I definitely heard them.

"Here's a pan. Go out and pick enough berries for a

pie or for our dessert tonight," my mother told me. I looked at the enormous pan and knew I had to fill it to the brim to satisfy her. At least there were lots of berries in the field and it shouldn't take long. I went out to the side of the yard and stepped through the hole in the barbed wire fence. I stood up, took a deep breath to get up my courage, and boldly marched into the snake pit, or rather, berry patch.

I began turning back leaves, looking underneath for clumps of berries. Oddly, there weren't any. Only a few old hard ones that hadn't ripened. The sun was hot and sweat trickled down my arms and back. I knew mother was going to be angry if I didn't show up with a full pan. I kept looking.

Finally, I had exactly seventeen berries. They didn't even make one layer on the bottom of the pan. They rolled around easily as I tipped the pan first this way then that. What was I going to tell mother? I knew the truth would sound like a lie.

"But, Mom—" I whined. "There aren't any—there really aren't any!" I could tell she didn't believe me.

"You're just too lazy to find them. Now go back out and don't come back until the pan is full!" she said angrily.

I knew it. She was going to be mad. I trudged out of the house—disheartened. You can't pick berries if there aren't any, I argued to myself. I combed the berry patch. The sun got lower. I didn't know what to do, only that I couldn't go home with an empty pan. The injustice of it all. Parents! I wandered listlessly back and forth across the patch, cursing my bad fortune. Even the threat of snakes took a back seat compared to the problem of manufacturing berries out of thin air. I hated berry picking. I hated that patch. I hated Mississippi. I hated the Air Force. But most of all, right now, I hated my mother. Why didn't she come out and try picking berries herself? Then she'd find out. Find out there aren't any. No, she never picked them. That was my job. Well, there aren't any, there just aren't any, I kept telling myself indignantly.

Suddenly my mother was right there behind me. At first I thought it was a snake rustling through the leaves. I don't know which I feared more at that moment, snakes or my mother.

"There aren't any berries," I said, timidly, pleadingly.

"Well, I'll be darned," my mother said, looking briefly for herself. She turned to go, and I followed her back to the house, weary with my fruitless afternoon.

"Those white trash down the road must have picked them when we were away Sunday," my father said to her later that evening at dinner.

I sat there poking the food around on my plate. It would have helped if she had said she was sorry, I thought. I wasn't being lazy. I tried to be good, most of the time. I guess parents don't have to admit to being wrong. Only children have to do that. I stared at her, trying hard to read her mind. No, she wasn't sorry.

Jane began writing about a memory of frustration with berry picking and ended up writing about her anger with a mother who would not believe her and then would not apologize. Writing this paper was the first step in remembering the dysfunctional family she grew up in and how it had affected her life. In later papers Jane wrote about how her parents didn't believe her when she told them she didn't want to ride her bike to school because of the Brahma bulls who would chase her down the dirt road. That paper ended with this reflection: "I grew up stoically enduring fright, pain (a broken arm: they waited three days before taking me to a doctor because they didn't believe me when I said it hurt), sadness at being uprooted from place to place, and, developing through the years, an overwhelming anxiety. I learned to hide my feelings. Eventually, I told my parents nothing and they stopped laughing."

Jane's isolation eventually led to her nervous breakdown. She wrote one paper about her first night in a mental institution. No subject was too large for Jane's pen. She continued writing and with each new essay her written memories were reconnecting her with herself and the world. Several of her pieces were eventually published in a local women's magazine and Jane, who thought she was not a writer, went on to receive her Master's degree in Poetry.

When we write we begin to find clues in our past. Look through your notebook for memories, feelings, thoughts that want to be written about. Follow them like a hound fresh on the scent.

Triggers

- Pick a piece of your chart, your list, your cavewriting or snapshot and freewrite about it for ten minutes.
- Write down your earliest memories in short descriptions trying to recreate the memory in as much vivid detail as you can. Think of each memory as a picture postcard you are describing to someone with their eyes closed.
- Make a list of important childhood/adolescent memories. Pick one and freewrite about it for a page. Here are a few prompts: first kiss, cars, sex, insecurity, rites of passage, worst teachers, best teachers.
- Cavewrite early memories. Try to include as much detail as possible. Color them with crayons. When you're done try writing snapshots with words of those pictures. List memories of a childhood injustice. Pick one and freewrite about it for ten minutes. Stop and write your adult reaction to this memory.
- Write about: A time someone hurt you
  A time you hurt someone
  A time someone helped you
  A time you helped someone
- Write about: A first time you attempted to do something
  A moment of childhood insight
  A moment a prayer was answered
- Print your name on a piece of paper. Cut it into letters and rearrange it. Try writing an acrostic poem (each line starts with a letter of your name).

Example: Born
All
Ready
Ripe
Yesterday

- Write a poem that begins with the words, "Inside me. . . ."

Think of a landscape, a place or a thing that could be inside you.

Don't be literal. Let your mind expand with the possibilities.

• Write down five unspoken rules of your family.

• Write a snapshot of an everyday childhood moment like this one by second-grader Delia French:

> My supper is always the same.
> My sister won't eat.
> My parents get upset.
> My other sister whines.
> But I just listen to the crickets.

Express Letters

Writing letters is another, more direct way to re-remember our childhoods. An *express letter* is simply a letter that expresses what is in our hearts. Here's how it works.

Think of a friend you loved or a parent. The person can be alive or dead. Write that person an express letter. It should contain at least one thing you have never before expressed. Don't feel compelled to mail the letter, just write it. Write quickly. Allow your thoughts, feelings and ideas to emerge before you think about them.

Read back your letter. Look for things you didn't expect to write. Circle parts you like. Read the letter out loud and imagine the person is beside you. Write down one feeling that seems to summarize the tone of your letter.

Digging Deeper

Which experiments worked best for you? Why do you think so?

Did you uncover any new feelings or new details as you wrote, or did it all go as expected?

A Letter to Yourself

Lee was a prisoner who discovered the power of letter writing over phone calling. Lee observed that if he was angry at his wife and wrote a letter, the anger would be gone by the time the letter was written. He would look at the letter the next day and decide not to mail it, because his thoughts were no longer clouded by irrational feelings.

Unfortunately, the same was not true of Lee's phone conversations with his wife. These were fraught with endless arguing. He realized that the power he learned through writing did not carry into his everyday life. When we make a phone call we talk to another person. When we write a letter we talk to ourselves.

Triggers

• Here's an exercise for seeing the power of writing to look back on feelings. Write a letter to a friend you haven't seen in a long time—yourself, years ago. Think of a time when you were feeling down. Write a letter to yourself back then.

• Write a letter to an old friend who you lost touch with. Describe what you know now about your friendship and life that you didn't know then.

• Write a letter of praise to yourself. For fun, mail the letter to yourself. Open it up and read it. Carry it with you for a day or two.

• Write a letter of complaint to the manager of the universe.

• Write a letter to the leaders of the world. Give them your opinion about how things should be handled.

• Write a short note to yourself expressing one harsh truth about your life.

If Only You Were Perfect: Make Your Awkwardness Work for You

OK. Maybe you've been trying to do some of the exercises in this chapter and you say to yourself: I'm no writer. There's nothing deep happening here. I hate this stuff I'm writing. You have doors closing in your mind, eyes red-penciling your thoughts. Stop. Pause. Take a few deep breaths. . . . Tell yourself this: "I don't have to be perfect. I don't have to write perfectly. I am alive and I have something to say. No one and no voice is gonna stop me."

The best writing advice I've ever heard came to me via my friend, Geof Hewitt. Geof is a poet who teaches in schools. When students are stuck, he paraphrases poet David Ray and tells them to make their awkwardness work for them. If you can't describe the beauty of a tree, write about how you can't describe the beauty of a tree. Express your confusion, your fear, your bewilderment, your anxiety. Let it come out of you. Let it spill and dribble onto the page.

I don't want to write about my father. Whenever I start, I feel pain and confusion. I am writing this at my mother's house. There is a photo of him on the wall in front of me. He is wearing a tie and a dark suit that blends into the background. My mother stands beside him dressed in black, and her dress also blends into the background and her thin gold chain seems to float on the surface of the photograph. They both look serious, but my father is about to break into a smile. It's one of those dumb smiles he liked to make whenever he played with young children. I see my father playing with Jessie, my daughter. I see him with that same smile in the doorway to the kitchen. My father's childhood was filled with pain. His father died when he was five. Once he told me how he watched him die and they laid him out on the kitchen table with candles at either end of his corpse. I remember the pain in his voice when he told the story, but there was also a playfulness. "I didn't know what was going on. I was just a kid."

In some ways my father grieved for his father his whole life. And as I write about my father, I feel like I am grieving for the grandfather I never knew. My father is more than the memories and ideas I have about him. I need to go beyond them, see inside them, find the truth under the shadows.

If childhood was a dream, when I write I wake myself up.

Speak Memory

With any luck your pen is teaching you to remember. We have explored techniques to open up the warehouse of information stored in our minds and to help get some of the goods onto the paper. It is a long complex process. But if you have surprised yourself even once with an old memory that jumped onto the page, perhaps you are beginning to see, despite all the odds, why writers need to write and how writing feeds them.

The next chapter focuses on how we grew up. We learn techniques to begin questioning our past to see the link between who we were and who we have become.

▪ Chapter 2 ▪

Questioning Memory

A book should serve as an axe for the frozen sea within us.
— Franz Kafka

I n David Mayberry Lewis's TV series "Millennium," a chief from a tribe in the Amazonian rain forest touched on the heart of all writing when he said: "Life is about asking questions."

If I were asked to describe a writer in five words or less, I would use this same concept: " a person who asks questions." Natural curiosity is the fuel of all powerful writing and is also the best tool for discovering what's important and what wants to be written about. Writers develop habits of seeing beyond the obvious to find a deeper focus and meaning and to discover new directions. Questions reflect our awe, confusion, excitement, joy, sadness — our engagement with the world. When we write as experts our words are boring, but the moment we show our ignorance, our curiosity, our vulnerability, our words become engaging for both ourselves and the reader.

Writing Is Digging Potatoes

My most current model for the writing process is the potato plant (see the facing page). Much of what we write is the leaves and stem of the potato. But the more we write and learn to search for meaning, the more we dig up potatoes. What's a *potato*? A potato is an unresolved question, a memory that asks to be written about, a person or place or event that has haunted your memory for years, a crazy idea you love to think about, a smell or a song that triggers a thousand memories. In short, a potato is anything that makes you want to write so much you can feel it tugging at your pen. In elementary schools I can tell the students who have found potatoes. They are the ones who don't look up when the bell rings, who sit passion-

30

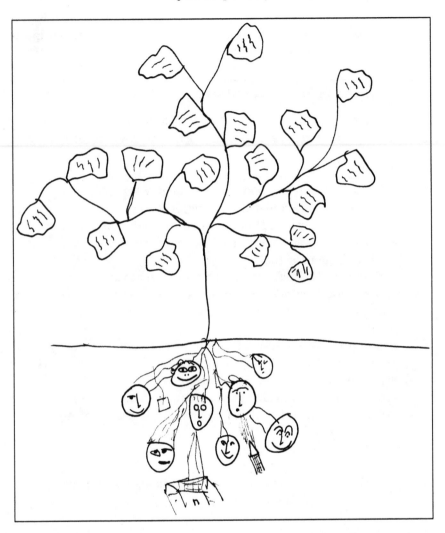

ately scribbling. But oftentimes writers don't find their potatoes till they begin writing.

In Chapter 1 you began to let your pen remember childhood memories. With any luck, you unearthed some memories or feelings you thought you had forgotten, or found an old feeling attached to a place or person. You began returning to your past and you learned a few techniques to explore your ideas without being chained to writing a story or essay or any other particular form. In this chapter I show you ways to begin digging for potatoes in the past, using questions as spades.

Growing Leads From Questions

You look out the window, and you see the tip of a tiger outside, and you know there's a whole tiger attached to that tip, and you wonder about the tiger.
— Mekeel McBride

Writing leads is a great tool for digging a potato in a piece of writing. A *lead* is a journalistic term for the beginning of any piece of writing. Writer Paul Horgan calls the lead the "organic seed from which all that follows will grow" (*Shoptalk: Learning to Write With Writers*, Heineman, 1989).

Strong leads pull the reader and the writer in and raise questions in the reader's mind, questions that often contain the essence of what lies ahead. Strong leads dig up potatoes for us to wonder about.

Listen to the questions that stir in your mind when you read these leads. What is the thing you want to know more about? I've written mine in italics beneath each quote.

- Looking back to all that has occurred to me since that eventful day, I am scarcely able to believe in the reality of my adventures. — Jules Verne
(What were your adventures?)

- His boot felt empty without the knife in it. — S.E. Hinton
(Why did he keep a knife in his boot?)

- The world as we knew it ended for us on a Tuesday afternoon in May. — Lois Duncan
(Why did it end?)

- I stand here ironing, and what you asked me moves tormented back and forth with the iron. — Tillie Olson
(What did you ask?)

Notice how a strong lead engages your natural curiosity, gets you wondering about the potato, points the writer and reader in a direction. Realize that the questions in your mind as a reader probably popped up in the writer's mind after the sentence was written.

I've developed a useful technique for finding strong leads that pull in both the writer and the reader. It's called *growing leads*. Here's how to do it.

1. Think of a time you were scared, embarrassed, hurt or confused. List a few times or make a web chart about one feeling.

2. Freewrite for ten minutes telling the story from beginning to end.

3. Put it aside. Go for a walk or read a book.

4. After a few hours or days away from your story, try to read it as if you have never seen it before. What questions naturally arise in your mind as you read? Write down several questions that grow out of your own natural curiosity. (If you are in a writing group, ask people in your group to write questions about your story on scraps of paper and hand them to you.)

5. Imagine that each question is like a string attached to your pen. Some strings are slack, others pulled taut. Read over your questions, picking the two that pull most. Turn them into leads simply by answering them in a sentence or two. For example:

How did I feel when she told me about Grandma?

There was a lead brick stuck in my throat. I just stood there frozen, afraid to talk, afraid to feel.

6. Pick the lead you like best and continue writing for another ten minutes.

Digging Deeper

Which freewrite was more interesting? Why? Which lead did you like better? Why? Could you feel a potato pulling you to write further, or did your lead sputter out and die?

Mrs. Carberry Never Stopped Shaking Me

The more you write about your life, the more you develop an instinct for what is important. Professional writers learn to hone in on their excitement for any given subject. And, like potato gardeners, our main concern is always what is growing under the surface of our stories. Here's an example of potatoless prose. "My grandmother is 5 feet tall and weighs 120 pounds. She is from Brooklyn, New York, and worked in a shoe factory." Now let's dig a potato.

"I was ten years old the day my grandmother told me about how she met my grandfather in a shoe factory. She was a switcher and he was a set-up man."

Notice how the second lead is fueled by the writer's interest, whereas the first one appears to be a simple objective listing of facts.

Questions are like spades; they help us find the big potatoes that often elude us in our first drafts.

Here's a story I told to a group of third-graders recently. It's about being shaken by my kindergarten teacher. Maybe some of you have had the same experience. As I tell it, think of questions you could ask me.

> Mrs. Carberry was my kindergarten teacher and she had a bad habit. She used to shake kids when they didn't know the answer. Some of the kids called her The Carburator. I had never been shaken nor did I ever think I would be. I was a shy kid who tried to stay on top of things. I lived in fear of being called on and tried not to draw attention to myself. But one day, after I had been out for a week with the flu, I had my moment. Mrs. Carberry was holding up an oak tag card. It had a word on it that I was supposed to know, but I didn't know it. She asked me to come up to her desk. I remember this like it was yesterday. She wore a blue dress with tiny white snowflakes on it. As I moved closer her shadow seemed to rise over me like that of a mountain. Behind her were the mimeographed bonnets of Pilgrims that we had colored the week before. She swiveled in her chair into shaking position and I felt her hands grip both of my arms above the elbows. Then she started shaking and I thought to myself, "This is it. I'm being shook. This is not so bad. Why doesn't the answer come?" Then I had this hollow feeling at the back of my head and I could feel my eyes fill up with tears but they wouldn't cry.

I ended my story here and asked the third-graders to ask me some questions.

> How big was Mrs. Carberry?
> Why didn't you know the answer?
> Why did she pick on you?

When did she stop shaking you?

Any question can be turned into an opening or lead simply by answering it. This is what I was teaching the children. Finding a strong lead can be the best technique for getting to the heart of what you want to explore in a piece of writing. I picked the fourth question (when did she stop shaking you?) because it seemed to tug at a potato deep inside me as soon as I wrote it on the board. Here is my lead:

> "Looking back on that day now, I realize that Mrs. Carberry has never stopped shaking me. Whenever I'm faced with a situation where I have to know an answer, I don't feel confusion; I feel fear. I am back in the tiny kindergarten class with the bulletin boards full of Pilgrim bonnets and turkeys that they made us color in. Mrs. Carberry's hands are locked around my arms and she is shaking my body as though a current of electricity were running through us both. That was the moment when I learned that answers were more important than questions."

I had never thought much about that moment in kindergarten until a third-grader asked me that one question: "When did she stop shaking you?" Suddenly, other moments when I didn't know the answer later in life connected themselves to that same feeling. I remembered forgetting the notes at a violin concert in fourth grade, flubbing a speech in college, failing a driver's test and even getting a critical note from an editor about a manuscript. Always there is more than simply disappointment or anxiety. There is that frozen feeling at the back of the head. Fear. Remembering Mrs. Carberry helps me to get a handle on one source of that fear. As I begin to write about Mrs. Carberry and that one awful moment, I begin to understand why I remember that moment.

The right question is a key to unlocking the mysteries of the past.

Triggers
- Go through your freewrite and find another compelling lead. Write it at the top of a blank page and continue for another ten minutes.

- Write compelling leads to books you will never write. Have fun whetting the reader's appetite. Notice the fun of writing a lead that makes you want to write more.
- Write a lead to your autobiography. Don't start with, "I was born in _____." Instead find a moment in your life that defines you and start there.
- Write questions about any subject you remembered in the last chapter. Pick the best question. Turn it into a lead and keep going.
- Read these questions and answer them with leads. Pick one that intrigues you and write on.

> Who are you?
> When did you become an adult?
> Why don't you write?
> How do people change?
> Who were you?
> Is the night sky the same as when you were a child?
> What's a dream you have?
> Where do ideas begin?
> Who will you be?

- Write five questions about yourself aimed at revealing harsh truths. Try answering one with a lead.

The Unsentimental Education: Digging Potatoes in the Past

Knowing how to ask questions and growing leads from them is the first step in uncovering a deeper meaning in our experience. If I told you to brainstorm a list of all the people in your life whom you learned things from, where would you begin? Would you start with Mrs. Carberry, the kindergarten teacher you nicknamed "the carburator" because of how she tried to shake the answer out of you? Or, would you start with Johnny Phipps, the friend who taught you to blow smoke rings with the Taryton cigarettes he stole from his sister? Would you include your mother, who taught you how to sew and to hide your feelings? Or, would you write about your sister, who first told you about the birds and bees and how to pretend to ignore the boys you liked? As you brainstorm your list, don't think too much about what the people taught you. Let yourself remember and trust that what you remember is important. Stop when you reach twenty-five people. If you're having trouble remembering people, answer some of these prompts:

Who was your biggest influence?

Who was your first love?

Who were you afraid of?

Who comforted you?

Who were the bringers of joy?

Who made you laugh?

Who made you feel important?

Who beat you up and who did you beat up?

Who was the mysterious person?

Who did you admire? Who admired you?

Who was your best friend? Who was your worst enemy?

Who was your biggest nightmare? Who was your greatest dream?

Who loved you? Who did you love?

Who feared you? Who did you fear?

Pick a person off your list who wants to be written about and do a web chart of that person's influence on your life. Webbing, as we learned last chapter, is a shortcut to meaning. It helped me to remember people I would have overlooked with just a list. After you've made your list, circle the details that make you want to write. Pick one and begin writing. Freewrite for twenty minutes.

Digging Deeper

What surprises you in what you wrote? Did you remember anything new about your person? Why do you suppose you chose this person to write about? If you don't know, does your writing begin to tell you?

Remembering the Lesson of a British Shopkeeper

When I answered the question, "Who was the mysterious person?" Laurie Lawrence popped into my mind. Laurie Lawrence was a storekeeper in the town where I lived in southern England. I still remember him describing the sound of a bicycle with no tires riding over a cobblestone pavement in newly liberated Amsterdam. It's like an image from a film that plays over and over in my mind whenever I think of World War II. Recently, I heard that Laurie had died of a heart attack and a month ago I found an old photograph of him standing in front of his store. I don't really know why I started writing about him. All I know is that he wanted to be written about. I started brainstorming a list of details about him.

Bald
red hair
blue eyes
never married
his sister, Mrs. Hunt, owned the candy store
loved television and old movies
seemed like life itself was a movie
loved American actors — John Wayne
lived life in the third person
black bananas and everything rotten and overpriced
why did I shop there?
kind, afraid, angry?
injured
by what?
the story he told about the German pilot
tweed coat
walking the town late at night
that sleepy distant look in his eyes.
once told me that Christmas was a lonely time
so polite
so scared
stories of the old cinema
loved old movies
like a ghost walking through the town.

Next I did a quick freewrite about my subject.

I would go to his shop on Tarrant Street in the early morning when the mist was rising from the river in rich brackish clouds of steam. Sometimes I would stop for a minute or two and watch the flock of swans feed under the stone bridge, or Mr. Barrett, the old mullet fisherman, troll with his long bamboo pole. I was a young man, alone in a foreign country for the first time, and I was intoxicated with the newness of everything. The smell of coal fires burning, the old ladies with their bicycles and shopping carts, the heavy coins rattling in the pockets of my baggy pants as I walked down a street that was first paved by the Roman legions.

I met Laurie Lawrence my first week in England when I was still looking for a place to stay. He was a large, bald-headed man who sat behind the dusty counter of his old grocery shop like a king holding court. Behind him were shelves of cans and packages of ancient biscuits. He directed me to a bed and breakfast on Tarrant Street and invited me back to chat about America. He liked Yanks, "that's what we call you lads over here." He wanted to talk to me sometimes about "those wonderful films you've been sending us for years." Even then I could hear the sadness in his cheerful voice, almost like an echo.

Sometimes, late at night, after the pubs had closed, I would see him walking through the town alone. He wore a tweed sport coat and a bowler hat and he walked with his head upright with exaggerated grandeur. My room was on the street and I would watch him from my window. I remember the scuffing sound of his shoes on the pavement, how he would turn his head slowly to each side as he walked, as though conscious of the whole town looking at him from behind the curtained windows. Once I saw him by the bridge. It must have been three in the morning. I couldn't sleep so I went for a walk. He was just standing there watching the green tide roll in from Littlehampton. I said hello to him but he wouldn't look up or even blink. I wasn't sure if he didn't see me or if somehow I didn't exist outside the context of his shop.

Mr. Lawrence's shop was more of a museum than a place to buy food. In the window were shrivelling Jaffa oranges, brown pears, dusty melons. Inside it was dark and the shelves were full of Cadbury bars, biscuits, jars of penny candy that had a dusty museum-like look. Everything was behind a dusty glass counter.

My freewrite ended here. I ran out of gas. Here are some triggers designed to provide you with more energy.

Triggers
- Write a dialogue between yourself and your person.
- Climb into the mind of your person and write a page of thoughts.
- Send your person to a place that disturbs them.
- Write a physical description of your person on a separate sheet of paper and insert it into your freewrite using an arrow.
- Have your person write a letter to a close friend. In that letter have them describe something about you.
- To find more people to write about, brainstorm a list of places and see which people it leads you to. Here are some questions that may trigger places in your memory.

> Where did you feel safe?
> Where were you scared?
> Where were you confused?
> Where were you angry?
> Where did you learn independence?
> Where were you trapped?
> Where did you think about death?
> Where did you think about God?
> Where were you loved?
> Where was the place of mystery?

Reflecting
Now that you've stopped freewriting, go back and reread what you wrote. Write a few questions that reflect on what you unearthed in your writing. Freewrite another ten minutes trying to answer one or all of these questions.

Digging Deeper
Did you uncover any new truths about your person in your free-write? If not, try asking questions and following the one that wants to be answered. If yes, ask yourself more questions about the new insight or simply continue writing and let the meaning be revealed.

Why Did I Choose Laurie Lawrence?

Here's the question I chose to answer: What did Laurie Lawrence teach me and why did I choose to write about him?

I still don't really know what Laurie Lawrence taught me. Earlier I said it was the stories about postwar Europe; now, as I write, I've begun to see it was much more personal than that. He was such a lonely person. Though he was not unattractive, he never married. He seemed to contain some deep injury that he never dealt with — that part about him walking the town at night alone. As I write this, I just remembered that a townsperson once told me that as a boy of nineteen Laurie had parachuted into Italy. It was an ill-fated military move and thousands of Allied troops died. Had men like Laurie, in true British fashion, suffered quietly for years, anesthetizing themselves with television, afraid to live life for the future because the past weighed so heavily?

His shop with all the rotting fruit and vegetables became a metaphor for the fruits of his life that rotted prematurely because he had no way of processing his pain.

As I write this I remember a story Laurie once told me in the summer of 1982. I had been working at a rowboat rental place on Arundel Lake, a small man-made pond on the far side of a castle. The lake had been created as a sort of moat in the twelfth century, and history told how the Cromwellian army drained the water out and ate the remaining fish when it laid seige to the castle in the sixteenth century.

At the start of the Blitzkrieg, when Germany still thought it could bomb during the day, a Messerschmitt was shot down above Arundel and the pilot parachuted into the forest above the lake. Laurie, a teenager who had not yet been inducted into the army, was the first man to find the pilot caught in a tree up in Hijourne Park, the wilderness area surrounding the castle. He had expected to see a mean villain but found instead a young nineteen-year-old man who was scared out of his mind. He was wearing a torn leather jacket and was bleeding from the forehead. He spoke in broken English when Laurie asked him some questions. Laurie asked him why the Germans avoided bombing any churches or cathedrals. He said they used them as markers to find their way toward London. They only bombed the country to get rid of any bombs they had left over. They tried not to hit anything. He was aiming for the lake.

I remember Laurie telling me he felt "sorry for the lad," and as he said that there was a tear in his eye. I didn't understand it at the time, but looking back, I think Laurie was grieving for his younger self, the self that went to war.

Standing back and reflecting helped me to dig deeper into memory and discover the answer to a mystery. We educate ourselves when we write down the lessons people teach us. Let your list of teachers grow for pages and pages and write about the ones whose lessons are buried in time.

Triggers

• Find a photograph of a person who has taught you many things. Paste the photo in the middle of a blank piece of paper. Fill the blank space with all the things that person taught you. Add quotes from your person (as I've done above).

• Make a time line of your life from birth to present. Mark the events that affected your education. Pick one and write about it, describing it in detail as if you were back there. Then stand back and write about it with your current perspective.

• Make a time line or list of every schoolteacher you remember. Try writing briefly about each one and what they taught you, positive or negative. Try writing them letters, either thanking them or telling them off.

• Brainstorm a list of all your friends whom you learned things from. Write what you learned next to the friend.

• Get a large piece of paper and make a large cluster with "My education" in the middle. Brainstorm quick lists of everything you've ever learned.

• Begin with the words, "When I learn I . . . ," and freewrite for ten minutes.

• Draw a comic strip of a lesson you learned starting with the naive you and working up to the lesson and aftermath. Make at least three boxes in your comic strip.

• Think of a room or a place you have known since childhood. Write about how that room or place changed through the years.

Digging Potatoes in Jobs

> *Work is worship.*
> — *The Bahá'í writings*

Working is our way of entering society. It weds us to situations, places and people we might not ordinarily meet or learn to live with. Remembering and questioning jobs can be a powerful trigger for probing our feelings and understanding our relationship to ourselves and the world we grew up in.

In this next exercise we dig for potatoes in jobs.

Finding Jobs

Make a list of all the jobs you have ever worked. Let your list grow chronologically or skip around. Number your list and challenge yourself to keep going when your memory gives out. Cluster when you get sick of listing. Try to include every job, even if it only lasted a day or two.

Here is my list:

1. Camp Winaukee, dishwasher
2. Kentucky Fried Chicken
3. Eastern Air Devices
4. The Westerner Cafe
5. The Clothing Factory
6. The New England Center, janitor

7. The Lunch Cart
8. The Tea Wagon
9. The Starving Chef, Pizza Hut
10. Hannon's Upstairs
11. Greenhouses in England
12. Renting rowboats in Arundel
13. Bed and Breakfast
14. Little People's Daycare
15. Codfish Aristocracy
16. Dolphin Striker
17. The Firehouse
18. Great Bay School
19. Teaching assistant, UNH
20. Continuing Ed, UNH
21. Writing
22. Special Ed Aid, Middlebury
23. Raymond
24. Carpentry with Jeff
25. Carpentry with Stephen
26. Fences with Gavin
27. Milking cows
28. Cooking, 1796 House
29. Head chef, Snookies
30. Artist in the Schools
31. Resource consultant
32. Prisons
33. Opening Doors Books
34. Writing for money
35. Inner Traditions
36. Castleton State College
37. Lecturer/keynote speaker

Now circle one job that wants to be written about and do a web of it. Pick one intriguing strand of your web and freewrite for ten minutes.

Digging Deeper

Why does this job stand out from the others? Who was the person you remember most? Why? What did you learn? Can you think of one particular day, or better, one particular moment that sums it all up?

Why the Clothing Factory?

I am stretching pink shammy fabric along a long flat table, pulling the creases out from one side while Gene pulls them from the other side. The fabric is slippery and the pink giraffes and hippopotami glisten under the harsh fluorescent light. Gene smokes a meerschaum pipe. He is in his forties with a graying beard. He wears green turtleneck captain's sweaters and talks with a heavy Brooklyn accent. He told me he was once a member of the Actor's Studio, the same class Dustin Hoffman was in. He was there when Dustin got his break for the movie, *The Graduate*.

Gene also tells me about his three failed marriages to movie actresses. His last wife tossed the contents of a bottle of ketchup at him right in the middle of Sardi's restaurant. She screamed obscenities at him. He tells this story with a strange quality of pride in his voice. I am not sure whether to believe anything Gene tells me. He is probably a compulsive liar. He is certainly an unapologetic male chauvinist. He enjoys telling stories too much to really tell the truth, but I am spellbound by them. I can tell he is glad to have nineteen-year-old, Mr. Innocent on January break from college working with him.

The factory makes clothes for oversized women. The sizes start at 2x and go up to 7x. Some of the tank tops are the size of small tablecloths. In the main room are twenty sewing machines. Gene and I are the stretchers. We layer the fabric back and forth on the long table as the fabric unspools itself. Then Phil, the owner, comes along with a cigarette dangling from his lips, holding a piece of chalk and the cardboard patterns. He traces the patterns, then Joe, an old man, comes along with a large jigsaw and cuts out the patterns. Rumor had it that Phil was burned out of his factory in Connecticut when disgruntled workers torched the place one evening. That's why they moved the business to this abandoned woolen mill in Dover, New Hampshire. He'd managed to save a lot of his warehouse material. That's why many of the blouses and shorts smell like smoked herring.

My mother is a tagger. I visit with her during my fifteen-minute coffee break. She tells me that Gene is a crazy person and I should not take anything he says seriously. We sit in a smoky room with all the machine operators, all women. One woman told a story of her ex-husband tying her to a radiator and stealing her car. She was a thin wiry woman and she tells the story with little emotion, puffing on a cigarette. Gene asks her for her ex-husband's phone number. He needs advice dealing with his ex-wife. The women scowl and hiss at him as the buzzer rings and they move back to work in the bright room.

I worked this job for three weeks and these vivid gritty images stick in my mind. I could go on and on, describing how the furnace would break down and how Joe, the janitor, and I would ride the freight elevator down into the dungeonlike basement. He had this special torch and had developed a technique for relighting the furnace, which he assured me was not too dangerous when done right. I remember crawling into a cavelike opening under the furnace and holding the flashlight while Joe performed his miracle of light.

If we judge knowledge by what we remember, I learned more at this three-week job than I did in all my years of college. How many jobs have you forgotten? What will they tell you when your pen remembers them? Who will jump out of your memory onto the page?

Triggers

• Write about one moment on a job that you loved. Make it a moment that expresses your love for the job, but don't write about your feelings. Let your love come through in your description.

• Write about your most embarrassing job interview.

• Go through your list of jobs and write one or two sentences for each job describing exactly what you learned. Think of moments or people on the job that turned into lessons.

• Write a resume which highlights all the reasons why you are not qualified to work anywhere. Cite specific examples to back up your assertion. Have fun.

• Write a letter of application to the perfect employer for the perfect job.

• Write about a moment of revelation on the job.

• Remember a time when you were humiliated on a job. Free-write for ten minutes, recalling the moment in as much detail as possible. Answer this question: What do you know now that you didn't know then?

- Write about your first day on a job. Recall smells, sights, sounds. Describe in detail those first impressions.
- Write a job resume to your best friend, including all the stuff that you would leave out of a real resume.
- Draw a cartoon or comic strip of something funny that happened to you on the job.
- Write a job description for your dream job. Then make a list of your qualifications.

Getting Fired

Getting fired is one of the most humiliating experiences a person can have. You feel pain, fear and sadness coagulating around a pit of anger in your stomach. You are suddenly invisible. People walk by you and seem guilty when they acknowledge your presence. You have been fired, sacked, terminated, bagged, canned, rift, axed, discharged, shafted. You have lost your job and that part of you that identifies with your work is in shock. You will carry that wound for a long time unless you write about it or find some other way of processing the experience.

Make a list of all the jobs you were fired from and freewrite a description of the reasons behind each firing. If you have never been fired from a job, think about what it might feel like or imagine yourself in the shoes of someone you know who was fired. How would it change your world? Try creating a character like yourself and have that person fired from your job.

I've been fired from three jobs: one as a janitor, the other as a university professor and the last as an editorial assistant at a publisher. How many jobs have you been fired from? If none, have you ever quit any?

Pick one job and freewrite about the leaving experience for ten minutes.

Digging Deeper

Did you remember anything new about your discharge? What did it feel like to write about that day? How has time changed your relationship to that event?

Rewriting Life's Injustice

> *I write to correct life's unfairness.*
> —*Verandah Porche*

I was a janitor/cameraperson at a conference center and was fired for failing to clean the toilets properly. I remember the director of the center calling me into his office and sitting me down next to him. He was a Harvard graduate and wore a gray pinstripe suit. "Barry," he said turning to me as he puffed on a pipe, "I'm afraid we're going to have to terminate the relationship."

"But Len," I replied, "we've been going together for such a short time."

That night I was supposed to videotape a group of fundamentalist Christians giving speeches about immortality. I was not in the best frame of mind as I sat there in the video control room operating the cameras mounted to the ceiling in the rooms upstairs. I very spontaneously decided to add a few visuals to the presentation. Each time a speaker mentioned the word *immortality* I opened the iris on the camera so that the speaker slowly began to dissolve. This was not the most mature response to being fired, but each time I played with the camera I could feel a part of me rejoicing in sweet revenge.

Looking back I can see this was an adolescent attempt to get back at the place that was firing me. But, like most attempts at revenge, it was fruitless. In the end, I only ended up getting my friend who ran the media center in trouble and I felt worse for letting him down. Truth is, I probably deserved to be fired from that job and I had little reason to feel I had been wronged.

But years later I was fired from a job for unjust reasons. I received a letter saying I was not going to be rehired as an instructor of English at the university where I had taught as an adjunct faculty member for two years. I wasn't exactly sure of the reasons, but I had a feeling they were partly due to political maneuvering which my colleagues and I had done on behalf of the adjunct faculty, and my unorthodox methods of classroom teaching, which were not always understood by other faculty in the department.

I had known other adjunct faculty members who had been dispatched in a similar manner. I remember the uncomfortable feeling I'd felt the year before when I had been rehired and others had not. Then, it had been explained to us that adjunct salaries were an embarrassment to the university, the method of hiring adjuncts was unfair, and the job had no security. The administration had done these people a favor by letting them go.

When my turn came I realized what bugged me most was the expectation that I keep my mouth shut and fade away, like my predecessors. I was out running one morning when I started composing an editorial about the fate of adjuncts like myself. It was called "Life on the Tenuous Track" and spelled out the plight of part-time instructors. As I wrote this editorial in my dark office the next day, each new sentence seemed to erase a little bit of my humiliation. I sent it to the student newspaper and it was published the next week. Here is the ending:

> I am writing for my colleagues in the English department who are also outstanding teachers but who are still made to wait in their offices for the letters to come out. I am writing for the part-timers in other departments here and at other universities across the country, who live from semester to semester on the fringes of departments that are too afraid and unimaginative to give them the respect they deserve. I am writing so they will get out of their offices and stand together in the hallways.
>
> Recently the part-time instructors at the University of Maine South Portland unionized and now the University must bargain with them as a collective force for pay increases, benefits and hiring procedures. They have the right to negotiate contracts and the right to strike. They are no longer isolated within their departments, subject to the whim of the Dean and Department Head. All it takes to begin the process is for ten part-time instructors to get together and form a bargaining unit. Ten people who are not afraid.
>
> Isn't it about time part-time faculty at this university got their act together and asserted the power given to them under the United States Constitution? Isn't it about time we joined hands instead of remaining invisible behind office walls?

My editorial helped me to realize that a good deal of my anger stemmed from the conditions I had worked under for the last two years, not the firing. I was a little disturbed that I hadn't written this editorial a year ago, that I had to wait until I had nothing to lose before I opened my mouth.

Writing can be the best way to break the silence that keeps people apart in systems that pretend to be beyond their control.

Triggers

- Try writing a letter to your boss, or an editorial about the injustices you witnessed where you work. Tell what's wrong and give suggestions for improvement. Let your boss know how you and others feel. Share your letter with someone. Remember, it was the process of writing it that was the most important. You are learning to question and you are turning your questions into answers.

- Describe the exact moment you knew you were fired. Where were you sitting or standing? What was going on around you? Try to fill a page with description. Don't write much about your feelings but let them come out as you describe the world around you.

- Create a character who has just lost a job like one you lost. Describe that individual's thoughts and feelings. Send the person for a walk to the bathroom; make that walk last a long time.

- Write the word *FIRED* in capital letters at the top of a blank page in your journal. Write a short poem describing something about a time you were fired.

> Example: Fired.
> The faucets in the women's
> bathroom didn't shine.
> Lipstick smeared tissue on
> the floor, hair in the sink.
> I am the janitor
> who lost his job.
> I am the janitor
> mopping up old memories
> with Spic and Span.

A Portrait of Memory

By now your memory has begun to tell you things. You have written about people, places, jobs. Your real stories are working their way to the surface. You are beginning to isolate and search for meaning in them. You have a few shovels and you know what potatoes look like.

Just for a break, try this: Get a large piece of blank paper and cavewrite a portrait of your memory.

Include drawings of experiences; key words; names and sketches of friends; questions you ask; and anything else, including photos, cut outs, etc. If you want, get a large piece of paper and let your portrait turn into a giant collage. Cut out magazine images and newspaper headlines. Mix them with photographs and memorabilia.

Look at your portrait. Revise it by adding more detail. Share it with a friend. Hang this chart in the room where you write. Look at it during moments of boredom. Think of the wonder in you, the undiscovered lands your pen can explore.

In the next chapter we will learn to see the patterns in our stories.

▪ Chapter 3 ▪

Core Stories:
Writing What We Need to Say

You don't choose a story, it chooses you. You get together with that story somehow. . . . You're stuck with it.
                                            —*Robert Penn Warren*

Psychologists who study addiction often talk about "core beliefs," patterns of thought that a client sees as the inescapable truth of life. *Core stories* is my term for something very similar. They are stories that demand we tell them over and over again, in different shapes and different forms. Many writers, such as F. Scott Fitzgerald, have remarked that they have one central core story that they repeat using different characters, settings and plots. Learning to identify the common themes and questions of our stories gives us insight into what may be our one core story.

Last chapter we learned to dig up potatoes, probing our memories for meaning. In this chapter we learn to compare and identify the potatoes that pop up in our stories and attempt to get a glimpse of our core story. The first step in identifying a core story is to examine the themes in the stories we tell.

For example, a theme in my core story is how I separate reality from fantasy. In Chapter 2 I wrote that Mrs. Carberry's kindergarten was a fearful place; yet I accepted it as normal when she shook me. My fear isolated me. I didn't tell anyone. I suffered and accepted abuse and pretended it was normal. Only in writing does my memory begin to sift the reality from the fantasy.

My friend Tom has a similar core story. Many of his stories have a moment of revelation in them in which Tom says to himself, "I can't believe this is happening to me. This is crazy." It's true. It doesn't matter whether he is describing the moment in college

R.O.T.C. when he was asked to fire on a dummy of a man and realized the insanity of war, or is recounting the dispute in a cafeteria he was managing where one of the workers took a kitchen knife and held it to his throat. That same line appears: "This is crazy. I can't believe this is happening to me."

Seeing the repeating pattern in our stories helps us to understand the patterns of the past and speculate about ways to intervene in the future. In this chapter I show you a few ways to begin identifying your core story, and to begin the process of digging deeper into the themes that connect it to your life.

Most of us likely have more than one type of core story. However, the more we examine them the more we see one central story emerging.

Finding the Core Story

Begin by listing several stories you have told over the years. Look back through your journal and find some potatoes, or stories, that intrigue and want to be told.

1. Get a tape recorder and record five of the stories.

2. Listen to the stories and write down one word or a short phrase that sums up the overall feeling of the story.

3. Look for similarities among the five stories and freewrite for ten minutes about what you think your core stories are about.

4. Write one question that still lingers in your mind about each story. Compare the questions and look for similarities.

Digging Deeper

Was it easy to tell stories into a recorder or was it slow going? Could you find patterns or themes in your stories or do they all seem different? Did old memories return as you told your story?

Is This Really Happening? My Core Story

I was sitting on the back seat of the EGGED bus, rolling down the Sinai Peninsula, when I noticed the Bedouin boy staring at me.

He was about fourteen years old with a haunted, nervous look in his eyes, which I interpreted as fear. It was January 1979 and Israel had suffered many car bomb attacks and one or two buses had been incinerated by the grenade launchers of Palestinian guerrillas. The day before in Jerusalem I had stood idly by and watched a group of Israeli soldiers standing around a white Mercedes Benz. That night on the news I learned they were dismantling a car bomb. The next day I found myself imagining cars blowing up in slow motion. I was traveling alone in a war zone. Looking back, I suppose I had a right to be suspicious of a Bedouin boy who kept staring at me in between sips of his bottle of Coca-Cola. But why me? Most of the other people on the bus were Europeans, from Sweden or some such Scandanavian country. They talked like they came straight out of an Ingmar Bergman movie.

They were traveling in a large group and I was the only outsider, me and the Bedouin boy. The fifth or sixth time he looked at me I did what any normal person would do when a stranger stares: I turned and looked behind me. That's when I saw the Jeep with the three Bedouin men, all wearing sunglasses and checkered affiyeh. I looked closer and saw what I knew were machine gun barrels sticking out from behind the back seat.

Stay calm, I thought to myself. There's nothing to be afraid of. You are imagining the whole thing. There is a Robert Ludlum thriller stuck in your brain. The boy looked at me again. He had just about finished his Coke and he seemed to be ready to spring toward the front of the bus. He's making his move, said the movie director in my head. This is it. He'll get off the bus, signal with his hand and they'll open fire.

Calm stay calm. Nothing is happening. You are imagining the whole thing, I told myself. The Swedish people were all laughing and telling stories. They were enjoying the scenery. Lambs to the slaughter.

The boy signaled to get off the bus. I knew it was time. I sat frozen in my seat. I did nothing. I said nothing. The Bedouin boy got off the bus. The jeep picked him up, pulled a U-turn and drove away in the other direction. Nothing happened.

I told this story to a group of high school students recently and they asked me some questions on paper. One jumped out at me: Why didn't you do anything? I didn't do anything because I didn't know anything was really wrong. In the back of my mind I knew the whole thing was going on in my head. But then again, maybe it wasn't. This is a theme in many of the stories I tell. I don't trust or know what is real and what is just in my head. Above all, I don't tell anybody that this is how I am feeling.

What themes do you find in your stories? One way to begin finding them is to begin by telling the meaning of your story in as few words as possible. Think of the tone or mood of your stories. After you've done a few, complete this sentence: "My stories are about . . ."

Triggers

• Write down the themes that run through the stories your parents told you.

• Cavewrite a theme in your stories.

• Make a list of old songs from your childhood or adolescence. Put one on the stereo and listen to it. Where does the music take you? What memories and themes arise in you?

• Find some old photographs of yourself. Look at your face and try to remember the situation of the photograph. What is the theme of the photograph? How does it connect with themes in the other photographs?

• (Group exercise) Act out a moment from one of your stories. Play a character other than yourself. Direct the other members of the group on how to play their parts.

The Story Circle

You don't have anything if you don't have the stories.
                                                    —Leslie Silko

Finding themes is a natural process that comes after we have told many stories. So let's tell a few stories. Invite family or good friends for a story night. You are going to teach them a native American ritual called the *story circle*. Western European society's ritual is called *conversation*. That's where you tell me about the time you totaled your first Chevy, and I butt in and say, "That reminds me of the time I wrecked my VW. . . ." With a story circle only one person talks—the person with the talking stick. A *talking stick* can be anything from a pen to an elaborately carved cane to an empty roll of toilet paper. I suggest finding an object that has some meaning to you. Once everyone is sitting in a circle, pass the stick around and have people start telling stories.

Here are a few prompts I've found to be wonderful for dredging up core stories and jump starting story cirles. Some of these contain themes that could be considered core stories in themselves. (Note: When issuing a prompt, always leave the storyteller the option of just telling any old story. The goal is to tell stories, not fullfill assignments.)

> A time you ran away (Note: This doesn't have to be just physically.)
> A time you escaped
> A first time doing something
> A time that was horrible then but you laugh about now
> The day you were no longer a child
> An encounter with death
> A time you did something you shouldn't have
> A time you did something you are proud of
> A time you were mystified
> A time you were confused
> A time you lost something (anything) forever
> A time you discovered something
> A time you were terrified
> A time something happened that confirmed something for you
> A time you were in awe
> A time you came home

• Each person tells a story; the others listen and write questions on scraps of paper.

• Questions go back to the storyteller and are put in an envelope for later.

Let the stick go round and round until everyone has told several stories. Explain to people that they don't *have* to tell a story when they receive the stick. But, ask them to hold the stick for a few seconds to feel if there is a story there. Because this is a circle the stick will come back to them.

1. When all stories are told, people look at their questions. Pick the question that pulls at you most and turn it into a lead by simply answering it (see Chap. 2). For example: "What were you doing there?" becomes "I didn't know what I was doing there."

2. Write for twenty minutes following the lead. Stop and reread what you've written.

3. Put your writing aside. Close your eyes and imagine the story you wrote about. Think of the place. Put yourself back there.

4. Open your eyes and list twenty details that you remember. A detail is simply a piece of information. It can be one word, like "Big," or a sentence or two, like "My father sits in the corner eating pistachio nuts and watching a heavyweight prize fight."

5. Stop. Look at your details. Make your details more specific by asking questions about each one to go a little deeper. Think of yourself as turning the knob on your binoculars to create a clearer picture. Write your revised details next to the original.

6. Pick one detail and on a new page in your journal freewrite about the event starting with the chosen detail. Let your pen stray from the subject if it wants to.

7. Reread what you've written and write one sentence that sums up a common theme between the two freewrites.

8. Write one question you still want to answer about your subject.

Digging Deeper

Are there any similarities between your questions? Did you discover any surprising details when you asked your questions? Did you uncover any common themes in your story that relate to other stories you have told or other events in your life?

Details Are Shovels

You don't write about the horrors of war. No. You write about a kid's burnt socks lying in the road.

—Richard Price

Finding our core story often requires digging deeper into our memories. This is not always a natural process for most people, but is a habit that writers develop.

The first morning I worked with Soeth we sat at a table in a small office. He wore a Boston Red Sox hat and white ankle-high sneakers. Apart from his complexion and accent he was an all-American boy. But when you looked into Soeth's dark brown eyes, the pain looked back at you. You knew he was from Cambodia and all the stories you'd read about and seen in movies were true.

I told Soeth the process of writing was the process of uncovering details, and that writers learn through writing to ask themselves questions that unlock more and more details until common themes emerge. Today I would ask the questions and he would make lists of details. We started with his village home, with the dirt floor, thatched walls and fire in the middle. We moved to the camps — ten kids in the bamboo building, ten-feet high, thirty-feet square; the sound of children crying for their parents; up at five and back to the camp at five; one meal of soup made of greens and fat; stabbing rats and lizards with sharp sticks and eating them raw.

Soeth's story came alive the more he told it and the more he wrote it. He wrote about running away to see his grandfather's funeral and returning to be staked up over a nest of red ants. He wrote about walking through mud flats full of skulls and bones and the endless stream of bodies floating down the river. And, as he wrote and re-wrote his story and allowed it to come alive with details, he knew it was somehow not just his anymore; it was something he could share.

Some people questioned Soeth's sense of reality because his stories kept changing. Soeth's inconsistency is true of any person who is struggling to bring to consciousness tragic events in their past. As we will explore in Chapter 6, storytelling is a circular process. So the more we do it, the more we discover what really happened to us — not simply objective facts. I believed everything Soeth told me. And the more I listened, the more permission Soeth had, with our help, to dig deeper into the painful memories he outlined in this sketchy draft.

> When I was six, a Kmer Rouge work camp leader took me away. I never lived with my family again. The camp was filled with little children, from ten to fifteen years old. I was the youngest. Usually the Kmer waited till a

child was ten before they took him away. My father let them take me when I was six years old. I had a fight with my little sister. Now I can't remember what the fight was about. The fight made my father very angry so he sent me to the camp. This wasn't his fault because he didn't know what was going on. This was the first time the Kmer Rouge came to collect children in the village. My Dad and I thought it was only for two weeks.

I was very disappointed in my father when I was at the camp but I couldn't do anything except cry out loud. The leaders made us work and told us, "If you work real hard you'll get to go home soon." So we worked real hard. But day after day you never got to go home. Finally I realized that we were never going home again.

The more Soeth's story unraveled, the more his theme of abandonment and confusion made itself known. Soeth's central question was not, "Why did the Kmer Rouge do this to their own people?" but rather "Why did my father do this to me?" As Soeth tells and retells his story, that question, with all its painful emotional undertones, makes itself known.

Keep looking for the common themes in your stories and you will begin to see the truth about the past.

Triggers

- Try finishing this sentence, "My stories are all about. . . ."
- Write about two times you were scared. Look for a connection. Can you detect a core story?
- Write about the day you changed.
- Write about a missed opportunity.
- Write about the day you became the person you are.
- One way to find your core story is to locate your big question. The next six triggers illustrate ways to play with that question.

1. Try writing a big question that seems to run through your stories. Cavewrite an answer to your big question.

2. Talk or write for twenty minutes about your big question. Tell about different times in your life when you felt the weight of the question.

3. Sit quietly by yourself in a comfortable chair. Chant or speak

your question over and over again fifty times. Let the question sink into your mind as you speak. Afterward, relax for a minute or two, then write a short poem that answers the question.

4. Write a letter to yourself answering your question.

5. Write a dialogue between your question and you that takes place at different times in your life.

6. Paint a self-portrait with watercolors or with words. Include the question in your painting.

The Power of Place

Remembering certain powerful places in our past can unchain a memory that contains a core story. Write down a list of places that you remember vividly. You can use the same list of questions you used on page 40 to help your memory.

Where did you feel safe?

Where were you scared?

Where were you confused?

Where were you angry?

Where did you learn independence?

Where were you trapped?

Where did you think about death?

Where did you think about God?

Where were you loved?

Where was the place of mystery?

Pick one and write a short poem about it. Don't labor over the poem. Think of yourself as a Japanese Haiku master who quickly sketches what is right in front of him.

Digging Deeper

Did you find a place with a strong feeling about it? What did it feel like to describe the place? Did any forgotten details emerge in your writing? What aspect of what you wrote do you like best?

Did you remember anything new about the place? What would it be like to go back there today? List two feelings you associate with that place. What images come to mind to illustrate those feelings?

The Courtroom

When Paulette wrote about the courtroom where she went to get a restraining order for her violent husband, she began with feelings and images of who she was then. When she finished the poem she realized it was not just about one isolated incident in her life. It was a core story about waiting for her life to begin.

Restraining Order

She recalled the richness of the smooth paneled walls,
the lush carpeted floor, rows of straight-backed chairs
lining one side, carefully positioned in front of the
foreboding bench, at a respectable distance.

Waiting, waiting

The vast chamber was empty except for herself and
the guard. They sat and stared at each other as the
large wall clock stared back.
Ten, fifteen, twenty minutes
and still

Waiting, waiting

Could she do this?
Would she have the strength
to carry out this action?
God, grant me the serenity to accept
the things I cannot change,
the courage to change the things
I can, and the patience to keep on

Waiting, waiting

The massive carved door
to the outer chamber
slowly opened.
On silent feet they entered,
sober faced,
three silver-haired women and a man.

Each climbing the stairs to their seat
perched above the near empty room below.
There was no more

Waiting, waiting.

At first glance this poem is simply about the intimidation Paulette felt while waiting in the courtroom. The waiting was symbolic of the long years of enduring an abusive relationship. We very rarely set out to write our core story. It sneaks up on us and we often see it after we have written it. Can you see your core story emerging in your writing?

Triggers

• What is one theme that reappears in your stories? Write it in the middle of a blank page and web it. Look for other stories in your web and write one.

• Write about a place you were afraid. Pretend you are back there and reexperience your fear in your writing.

• Write about a place in a dream. Recreate the dream with words. Draw a picture of the dream. Make a comic strip.

• Write one painful thing that has happened to you that you haven't shared with anybody. Hold on to this.

• Write about a place where you were alone. Don't say you are lonely. Just describe the place and let your feelings come out in the description.

• Write about a fearful time in your life. Explode a moment. Enter the fear. Return to that self and make the reader feel exactly what you felt, exactly what you thought.

• Draw a portrait of loneliness with words. Illustrate it with a drawing. Then draw a portrait of togetherness and do the same thing.

Remembering Secrets

We are all prisoners—we are locked up in our own story.
                                        —*Maxine Kumin*

Another shortcut to finding our core stories is to think of the secrets you have kept in your life, secrets you have never told anyone. At one of my first seminars I asked a group of teachers to write down a secret they had never told anyone. Three people promptly walked out of the room. Another three hands shot up. "Do we have to share them with anybody?" a young woman sitting in the front row asked. I paused for a moment, then said, "Only with yourself." Afterward, an older woman came up to me and told me about the time she was working as a switchboard operator in 1935. An emergency came through her line. A little boy was crying and saying his grandmother was asleep. She calmed down the little boy and asked him where he was. It was only then that she realized the boy was her son and her mother had died. She had kept that story inside her for forty-five years, until that moment.

Write down three secrets you have kept for years. Pick one and freewrite about it for twenty minutes.

Digging Deeper

What did you feel as you wrote about your secret? Who did you keep it from and why did you keep it secret all these years? What do you know about your secret now that you didn't know then?

Deep Water Runs Deep

I used to have a secret from my parents. It happened when I was twelve years old. We were at Lake Wentworth in Wolfboro, New Hampshire. My parents had never taught me to swim because they didn't swim. I had practiced on my own and that day, while my parents were snoozing comfortably on their chaise lounges, I swam out to the raft. I stood up on the gray wooden raft and I could feel my heart beating with excitement. Then I saw my parents sleeping and I started thinking that if they woke up and saw I wasn't around they would panic. So I plunged back into the water. As I started to swim back I could feel my muscles tightening and my arms grow heavier. My hands became shovels digging into the water instead of paddles keeping me afloat. Water ran up my nose and my eyes blurred with panic.

Tiny bubbles swarmed around me like insects hungry for the kill. I tried to shout "Help!" but each attempt was muffled by the mouthfuls of water. Then I saw a tanned white-nosed lifeguard paddling out to me with his red surfboard. "Just hold on," he said, "I'll pull you in." The pebbles were warm under my feet. And, as I stood up, I could feel the panic settling like lead. I walked to where my parents were sleeping and fell down asleep on the blanket, glad to feel the sun warm me. I told them about my swim twenty-six years later after I found myself writing about it in a classroom freewriting session. I realized that I've lived with this need to protect my parents my whole life and one way I did this was to keep these stories secret.

When I told them, I suddenly realized how absurd it was to keep this secret. Yet I knew there was a reason, a profound reason that had to do as much with them as with me. When we write best we dig up mysteries and each new detail is a new shovel.

Triggers

• Describe secret memories or return to those you've already written about. List details and make them come alive. Then think about why you've kept them secret and write about that.

• Return to a room you knew well. List details that you remember about the room. Pick one detail from your list and freewrite about it for ten minutes. Circle interesting sections and ask yourself why this room is important to you. Draw a picture of the room. Color it with crayons. Try to imagine who you were then.

• List details describing a person you've kept a secret from. Pick one detail and freewrite a description of them beginning with that detail and ending with the person finding out about the secret.

• Create a character with a secret similar to one you have kept. But make the character different from you. Write about that character in a situation where the individual is forced to think about whether or not to reveal the secret.

• Write a letter to someone you've kept a secret from for years. Don't worry about whether or not you need to mail it. Just write the letter and discover why you've kept the secret.

• Write down all your secrets in a small book. Hide it somewhere in the house. Wait a few months and look at the book. Write about the secret that wants to be written about.

• Make a list of details about a person or place. Go back over the list and ask yourself one or two questions to make your detail more specific. Draw a portrait of the person or place based on the prominent details.

Death: A Universal Core Story

Core stories are not unique to ourselves. Psychologist Carl Jung would say we have a collective unconscious that combines our stories with every human being who has ever lived. There are certain similar themes. Jung called these *archetypes* and used this concept to illustrate the commonality of all human experience.

We are mortal human beings living on a planet at a certain time in history. Death is probably the most common experience. Write about your first experience involving death. Write quickly, letting your thoughts and feelings spill onto the page. Stop. List details of that moment or cavewrite it.

Digging Deeper

Look at what you've written. How have your thoughts and feelings about death changed? How have they stayed the same? Cavewrite a portrait of death.

Good Grief

Amy Miller, a fourth-grader at C.P. Smith School, was devastated when her beloved grandmother died. She refused to eat and was having a very hard time doing her schoolwork. She went to see the principal, and they mutually decided she could come any time of the day to her office and write about her grand-mother in a special journal. The title page began:

"My grandmother's name was Laura He-lene August Miller. She is 76 years old and was the greatest."

The verbal disagreement of the last sentence speaks to the power of writing to awaken the dead. When we write, the *was* becomes *is*. On the next page is a snapshot

My grandmoths lagh was so funny you had to lagh at it it was so cute. She would always call me a love bug and I felt warm inside when ever she said that

Amy wrote about her grandmother in her special journal. Notice how Amy's writing reflects her profound love for her grandmother.

Until the day I visited Amy's school she had kept the material in her journal a secret between herself, the principal and her teacher. The assignment I gave the children that day was simple. Pick a moment in time when something very dramatic happened, something you will never forget. Now, explode that moment all over a page. Stretch it out. Make it go in slow motion. Amy picked the last time she saw her grandmother and she read it to the class during share time.

> I sit wondering thinking trieing to know what is going to happen. I wasn't sure what to think when my father walked somewhere and talked to a nurse then he said "Do you want to see your grandmother?" I said please. I walked through the long hall very sloly wondering what to say How I should say it. While I was thinking I glanced at a few doors that were open seeing people with tubes almost evrywhere I go to a door and opened it. I saw my grandmother with tubes on her arms face and almost evrywhere. I thought this couldn't be the woman instead or pale with her legs tired. It seemed like it was an hour since we talked I said I love you I though was that the right thing to say I was getting scared. She said I love you too then I felt very good but sad.

Something remarkable happened when Amy read her piece and asked for questions. Hands went up all over the classroom. Heather told her how great it was to hear her feelings because she had the same feelings when her grandmother died. Billy told her she was lucky to have had a chance to say goodbye to her grandmother. His grandfather wouldn't let anyone see him when he was in the hospital. He was still mad at his grandfather for not letting him say goodbye. More children shared their hidden feelings about death. "They told me he went away," said Kurt. "But when I asked where and could I visit him, they wouldn't tell me."

After class, Amy came up to me and said, "You know I didn't tell anybody about my grandmother because I was ashamed. I didn't know that they all had the same things happen to them."

Amy's story illustrates a common core story of life in a modern

Western European society. We have forgotton how to grieve. People often die alone in hospitals away from families. We view death as something unnatural and to be feared. Moreover, because people don't have a shared experience of grief they hold it inside, except for moments when they express it in some tangible way. Writing is one of the best ways to grieve because it is socially acceptable, and art is something that can be shared as long as it is not seen as therapy.

Triggers

- Write about a moment in your life when you were very aware of death.
- Make a list of people who have died in your life. Pick one and write a snapshot of the person when he or she was alive. Write a letter filling them in on what they've missed.
- Put death in the middle of a web chart and brainstorm a list of experiences off that nucleus. Circle one strand off your web chart and freewrite for ten minutes.
- Write for ten minutes following this lead: "Death is. . . ."
- Describe the death of a fictional person in the third person.
- You have just died. Describe a trip to K-Mart or some other place you visit often but don't think about.
- Paint or draw a picture of your spirit. Hang it close to your writing desk and look at it. Try giving it a voice.
- Imagine your death scene and write your last words. Oscar Wilde, remarking about the ugly green curtains in the room where he lay dying, said, "Either those curtains go or I do!"
- Imagine you will die tomorrow. Write a letter to someone in your family. Tell that individual about what really mattered in your life.
- If you have a camcorder try making a video presentation to be played at your funeral. Tell the people there exactly how much you loved life. Read your favorite poems or stories. Sing them your favorite songs. Create your own vision of who you were for people to hold in their hearts.

The Story of a Flower

My daughter made this story about the other day. It's called "The Story of a Flower" and it's shown on the next two pages.

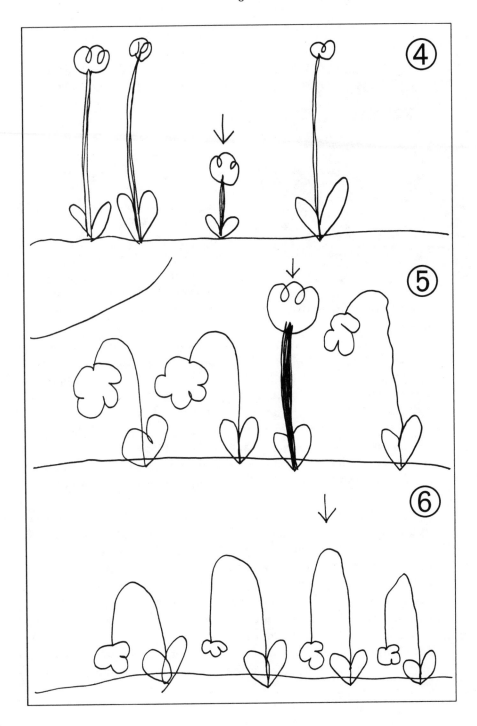

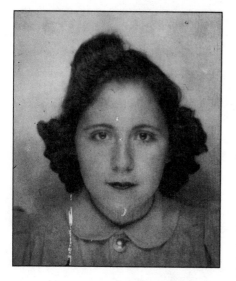

The arrow indicates the protagonist of the story, a flower who grows and dies slightly ahead of four other flowers who also grow and die. This is one of my daughter's first attempts to portray time passing and she does it the way most writers do, by putting a character in a context and showing a sequence of events.

Core stories are about time passing and people changing in fundamental ways. You can see stories in people's faces. On this page and the facing page are two photographs of my mother, one from 1940 and one from 1977. Can you see all the stories in her older face?

If I sat down with a tape recorder I could hear some of those stories. My mother would tell me about the anti-Semitism in the bank where she worked in Manhattan. She might tell me how hard it was to move away from her family in New York up to New Hampshire. She might describe her mother's death or the recent birth of her first granddaughter. She might talk about how worried she was when her kid brother went to Japan in World War II, or how frustrated she was having a son like me who seemed so lost all through high school and had now decided to drop out of college to wander the earth.

Writing stories is often the process of discovering those moments or events in life where we are somehow made conscious of ourselves changing. Significant moments don't reveal themselves to us until after we've begun writing about them. When I ask a class to write about an important event from childhood, invariably two or three students say they can't think of anything important. I tell them that whatever you remember is important, only you might not discover why until you've written about it for a while. Here are a few questions aimed at prodding your memory to dig up important moments. Read through them and make notes of memories they trigger.

What moment de-
lighted you?
What scared you?
What confused you?
What mystified
you?
What excited you?
What hurt you?
What made you
proud?
What made you lose
confidence?
What confirmed
something for you?
What made you uneasy?
What bored you?
What changed your life?

Digging Deeper

Which question stirred a memory of a moment? How did that moment change the way you think about yourself? What is the theme in that moment of change? Summarize that theme with one question. What was it like to return there and explode the moment?

Core Moments: Locating the Source

Returning to the big moments in our lives can be a powerful trigger for finding our core story.

Gerry is a convicted rapist who has been in therapy for two years and in jail for fourteen years. When I asked him to return to his childhood and write about a dramatic event from a child's point of view, he wrote the following short piece about an event that happened when he was seven:

The Ax

He had his hand on my branch. He has no right to my branch. If he does not take his hand off my branch I will chop his finger off. It is my branch. Get your hand off my branch. Do it now! You have your own branch.

This branch is mine. I have Dad's ax. I will use it. Do not dare me! I will do it. It is your fault! You did not take your hand off. I chopped his finger off. It has blood on it. I am in trouble. Dad will be mad. What can I do? The blood is all over. Run away! Get out of here. Hide the ax. It is Dad's ax. Why did I do that? He is all blood. I hurt him. I want to cry. I did not want to do it. I am afraid! Run away! Hide the ax. Do not know what to do. I will get a lickin from Dad! The cops will come. He is all blood. Stop yelling! Go home!

Looking back at this childhood voice from an adult perspective, Gerry could see that this incident was one of the first acts of spontaneous revenge for the daily sexual abuse he suffered as a child. The boy he attacked was an innocent bystander, one of his first victims. This pattern of heedless violence and then running away would lead him, as an adult, through three marriages and six prisons. Through writing and in his intensive cognitive therapy Gerry learned to return to previous situations and reexperience his life from a more mature perspective. Eventually he wrote this poem, which was eventually published by the National Coalition Against Sexual Assault newsletter.

If You'd Care For Me Then . . . Why Not Now?
I am a little boy who was kidnapped and molested for two days in a cemetery when I was seven or eight years old.

I am a little boy who was forced into oral sex, and sodomized by a neighbor friend for five or six years until the age of thirteen.

I am a little boy who was forced to masturbate and perform oral sex on a cousin at the age of seven or eight.

I am a little boy who was forced into oral sex, masturbation, and sodomized by my brother at the ages of twelve and thirteen.

I am a little boy with supressed feelings of shame, guilt and anger, hidden for years, resurfacing now and then, to pay the world back.

I am a little boy torn between two conflicting personalities: one of love, and the other revenge.

I am a little boy who ran all over the country, searching for happiness, in secret places unknown.

I am a little boy who escaped into a world of drugs and alcohol to lessen my loneliness and pain.

I am a little boy who was thrown into a boy's school to be abused even more.

I am a little boy who tried to be a Daddy to five lovely children, but failed.

I am a little boy who tried to be a husband to three separate wives, but failed every one.

I am a little boy who sexually assaulted two women, and was sentenced to prison for the past fourteen years.

I am a little boy who took it upon himself to find a way of healing himself of past abuse.

I am a little boy who never wants to hurt anyone else for as long as I live.

I am a little boy who still feels the abuse of these cold prison walls.

I am a little boy whom you would have loved and cared for at the age of seven.

I am a little boy who becomes confused and feels rejected when fellow survivors hate me.

I am a little boy who feels constant molestation of the mind when not understood by fellow survivors.

I am a grown man who has learned to forgive my perpetrators and open my heart to healing my revengeful thoughts.

I am a grown man who is paying his debt to society, and who now realises that the world can no longer be a victim for revenge.

I am a grown man who chooses not to be controlled by nightmares of past abuse any longer.

I am a grown man who is on the road to recovery, and understands that two wrongs will never make a right.

I am a grown man who can now cry, smile and care for others, and someday I will be free . . .

That little boy was me!

Returning to your childhood self and writing in that voice can be the first step in seeing the dysfunctional patterns of behavior that destroy our adult lives. No matter how degrading your life has been, identifying and expressing the core of that life is the first step in creating a new life.

Triggers

• Begin by drawing a line horizontally across a large sheet of blank white paper. Then make a thermometer-type graph with the horizontal line being point zero and the points above being positive and the points below being negatives. Now write *birth* at one end of your horizontal line and *death* at the other. Think of all the positive and negative experiences that have happened to you since birth and place them in their proper position on the graph. Draw or doodle little pictures to go along with your event. Make your graph a work of art.

• Pick a positive experience off your graph and freewrite about it for ten minutes. Pick a negative experience and do the same. Stop. Ask three questions about each freewrite. Pick the most compelling question and keep writing.

• Make a similar graph about one experience. Place positive and negative effects of one or two experiences on the new chart. Freewrite for ten minutes beginning with one of these effects.

• Write five snapshots of your mother and five snapshots of your father.

• Remember a family argument between your mother and father or your parents and you. Write it as a scene.

• Draw a family portrait putting in as much detail as possible. Then stop, look at the picture and analyze the relationships. Write a caption underneath.

• Write about yourself as a child through the voice of one of your parents.

- Write about a fictional family that is somewhat similar to your own family. Create a problem similar to one faced by your family.
- Get a large Spanish onion and sit in a circle with five close friends. As each person tells a story about their childhood they peel off a layer on the onion. When the onion is all peeled, freewrite for ten minutes about the stories you have heard. Share the stories.

Guilt and Blame: The Shut-Off Valves of Memory

Guilt, blame and shame stop us from sharing our own feelings with ourselves. If you are finding that your core stories are still hiding from you, try this: Draw a line down the middle of a page. Make a list of all the things you are guilty or ashamed of on one side. On the other side, write in a condemning voice that blames yourself for the thing you are most guilty about.

Freewrite for ten minutes answering that voice.

Digging Deeper

What did you discover about your guilt? Did you probe beneath it or is it still dominating your thoughts? Was it easy to add things to your shame list or did you find that certain events did not want to be remembered?

You Are Responsible for the Extinction of the Dinosaurs

There is a Jewish comedian named Gordon Godfried who does a wonderful routine on guilt and shame. He begins with the voice saying things like, "You never brush your teeth. You see. Your teeth are falling out. You see that. Just because you are so lazy." After rattling off several other condemnations the voice starts blaming the victim for larger historical events: "You are responsible for the French Revolution. Everything was going OK till you came along. You see. You had to spoil it. You are responsible. You are responsible for the French Revolution. And the dinosaurs. The dinosaurs were doing OK till you came along. You see. You are responsible for the extinction of the dinosaurs. They were fine until *you* spoiled it. You are responsible."

The more absurd the condemnation, the more transparent and silly the guilt-ridden voice becomes. Like the best humor, it creates enough distance so we can laugh at the absurdity of a human liability—in this case, guilt.

In real life, of course, guilt and shame aren't funny. When I look at my cavewrite of my father's death on page 20, I see that a part of me is ashamed of myself. I ask myself was I a good son? Did I let him down? Were there many things I shouldn't have said? Things I shouldn't have done?

A week after my father was gone I had my first dream about him. He was standing on the stair landing of the old house on Highland Street. He was a young man again, no more potbelly and a full head of black hair. He was wearing an old-fashioned white sleeveless undershirt and brown cotton pants. I was so happy to see him that I hugged him for a long time. "Daddy," I said. "It's so good to see you." I could feel his scratchy beard against my face, his arms gripping me. Suddenly, I have a thought. He's dead. I ask him. "You're dead, aren't you?" He nods quickly, silently, his eyes looking down at the wooden floor of the hallway. I wake up.

I felt relieved when I woke up. My sense of shame and unresolved feelings diminished. Somewhere my father was still alive. Somewhere he loved me, despite my flaws. You could say growing up is the process of accepting the reality of death into our lives and not letting it interfere with what we have to do here. Shame, guilt and other paralytic feelings stop us from expressing ourselves—stop us from living. Fear of anything is always fear of death. Abandon that fear and what is left? Perhaps this is the quintessential human core story. Let's write it together.

In these first three chapters you have remembered the past and learned to search for patterns and themes in the stories you tell. With any luck you have begun to discover your core stories and write them down. Maybe you are still in the process of remembering. That's OK. We are all different and we all have our own unique process for remembering. There is no right procedure, only many experiments. Don't despair if you haven't found your core stories. It is the process of looking that reveals them. We do much looking in the coming chapters.

Triggers

- Write about another event off your shame list.
- Write a soliloquy of shame to yourself. Capture the voice of

shame on paper. Stop. Reread what you have written and write a shameless reply.

- Cavewrite one shameful moment in your life.
- Draw a portrait of your shame in whatever way, shape or form you like.
- Write a children's story about a young child overcoming shame.
- Write a short poem with each line beginning, "I am ashamed of . . ."

Forgiving Ourselves

In the next two chapters we begin examining our stories and reframing them. Before we move on, however, I want you to try something. Look at your shame list. Pick the things you are most ashamed of and hold them in your mind.

Get a tape recorder and record your shameful story or simply write the story on a blank page in your journal. Wait a day or two and play back the tape or read the story. Pretend the story was told or written by someone other than yourself. As you listen or read, forgive the person telling the story. Write a letter to the individual or speak into the tape recorder. Read back or listen to your letter of forgiveness. Know that it is real. Let the burden of shame lift from you. Rejoice in all the new memories that lay hidden beneath.

Part Two

Reframing

Part of becoming a writer is the desire to have everything mean something.

— *Louise Erdrich*

▪ Chapter 4 ▪

Stale Roles:
Shifting Contexts
to Find Out Who We Are

We don't stop playing because we grow old, we grow old because we stop playing.
—Satchel Paige

ll meaning in our lives is created by a context or frame from which it emerged. Our sense of purpose grows from the situations of our past, be they family, society, race, religion, etc. Without self-examination we often live our lives responding to situations and events that happened years ago. Psychologist Harriet Goldhor Lerner, author of *The Dance of Anger* (New York: Harper-Collins, 1986), talks about the patterns of behavior we develop in our first family in order to survive. In successful therapy the client learns to create new patterns not governed by situations or contexts that don't exist anymore and responds out of a more authentic sense of self rather than the old expectations and stereotypes.

For example, Lerner teaches couples to use anger as an effective tool for gaining intimacy in a relationship. She points out that societal expectations discourage a woman's anger, labeling her a slanderous term like "bitch." (There is no real male equivalent to this term.) Once a woman begins to shed the negative stereotype associated with such a word, her anger can be a useful tool for getting her needs met and creating more intimacy with her mate. For men, learning to acknowledge and share feelings goes against the stoic context they grew up within. Labels like "wimp" keep them from exploring newer, more emotionally fruitful, territory.

You could say that self-discovery is the process of reframing our past. And, because writing creates dialogue between the present and the past, the conscious and the unconscious, it can be a powerful tool for doing this important work. In the next two chapters we play around with contexts and point of view to begin the process of reframing our past, present and future. Though our goals are very serious, our methods will be playful.

Gender Bending: Exploring Body Messages

This exercise works great with groups, or you can do it alone in front of a full-length mirror. Find some advertising circulars containing images of men and women. Underwear ads tend to work well, as do cigarette ads. Cut out a few and place them in front of you. If you are a woman, study the images of men first. If you are a man, study the female models. Notice the way the models stand, the expressions on their faces, their eyes.

Now, stand with your back to the mirror (or the audience if in a group). Count to three, then turn around and become the image of the opposite sex. Try to hold the same exact pose for ten seconds without laughing.

Next, turn around again and become a member of your own sex. Hold the pose for ten seconds.

While it's still fresh in your mind, freewrite for ten minutes about what it felt like to pose as a member of the opposite sex.

Defining Gender

Now that you've shifted gender contexts try this one.

Pretend you have just been hired by the World Book Encyclopedia Company to write a succinct but meaningful definition of men and women. You have been chosen not for your scholarly insight, but for your down-home wisdom and general good nature. You have the wisdom of the woman or man in the street. Write your definition in whatever form you feel will get your ideas across. You can freewrite it, write express poems, cavewrite, etc. The editor would also like you to illustrate your definition with drawings or cut out collages from magazines.

Digging Deeper

Which sex role was easier to write about, your own, or your other? In what ways have you rebelled against your own sex roles as portrayed by the ad? In what ways have you complied?

How does your definition differ from society at large? How is it the same? How does your definition grow out of your own personal experience as a man or woman?

The Mothers of Men

The world of humanity is possessed of two wings: the male and the female. So long as these wings are not equivalent in strength, the bird will not fly. Until womankind reaches the same degree as man, until she enjoys the same arena of activity, extraordinary attainment for humanity will not be realized; humanity cannot wing its way to heights of real attainment.

— *'Abdu'l-Bahá*

When I used to teach college freshmen the far-reaching importance of feminism and its effect on our lives I'd begin by reading them the definition for *Woman* from the 1968 *World Book Encyclopedia*, which opens: "There are many differences between men and women beyond the primary fact that women are the mothers of men." The entry maintains this condescending tone throughout and characterizes women as emotionally different than men, stereotyping them as only concerned with personal needs and desires and therefore more interested in social welfare than in science.

Everyone in the class would agree on the condescending nature of this entry. This, I tell them, is the context from which feminism emerged. And to a large extent, this is what most women are still up against. Then we tried to look up *Man* or *Men* in the same encyclopedia. There is no definition, only a brief, but very telling cross reference: *Man: See Human Being*.

The 1987 World Book entry for woman reflected a different context for women. It was written by a woman sociology professor from City University of New York. Her name and short biography were on the opening page. Instead of one picture of a woman hemming a skirt with her daughter, there was a small collage of images: a woman welding, a woman teaching, a woman in management and a woman holding a child. This definition stressed a woman's varied roles and had a much greater awareness of the varying treatment of women in different societies.

As women define themselves they create a new identity. Earlier definitions, which limited them, are placed in a new broader context casting light on the society that attempted to define them, not their own nature.

But what do we find when we look up *Men* or *Man* in the 1987 *World Book Encyclopedia?* You guessed it: *Man: See Human Being.* So I look up *Human Being:* "Man has the highest developed brain of any animal." Well, how much progress can an encyclopedia make in 20 years?

Yesterday, I found a 1991 *World Book Encyclopedia.* I looked up *Woman.* You'll be happy to know what I found: *Woman: See Human Being.* Now, that's evolutionary progress: from woman to human being in twenty-three years.

Our sense of self as a man or a woman does not have to be defined by the time that we live in if we know how to stand back and examine ourselves outside the context society creates for us.

Look at your freewrite and your definition. Which parts reflect your own definition through your own experience? Which reflect society's definition? Know the power you have to break models and create a new role for yourself.

Triggers

• Write a letter to your son and daughter (whether you have one or not). Tell them about sex roles and how to deal with them.

• Divide a piece of paper in half. On the top cavewrite stereotypes about your gender (use cut-outs from magazines as visual prompts). On the bottom half cavewrite images of who you are. Add questions about the disparities between who you are and the messages you receive daily.

• Pretend you are a highly evolved human being living 1,000 years in the future. You have returned to the twentieth century on a historical fact-finding mission. In a letter to your futuristic audience, explain the peculiar sex roles of men and women.

• (For men only) Find some makeup, lipstick, mascara, rouge. Put it on in the privacy of your own home. Look in the mirror. What does it do to your face? Write about what it felt like?

• (For women only) Find several images of a woman's face in magazine ads. Stare at them awhile and try to imagine the face without the lipstick, without the eye shadow, and so on. If you are a woman who wears makeup regularly, try this: Apply makeup to only half your face. Use a mirror to study the difference in the two halves. Write about it.

• Collect three male or female TV characters. List them on a blank page in your journal, leaving space beneath each one. Now describe what stops them from being real.

• An ode is a poem that praises. Write an ode to men or an ode to women. Your poem can be as sarcastic or as serious as you want.

• Think about the qualities you admire in men and women. Write a list of ten guidelines for being a real man or a real woman.

• Close your eyes and take several deep breaths. Imagine a world where men and women are truly equal. Freewrite about what it's like to live there.

• Cavewrite all the stereotypes and clichés you can think of about your sex. Pick one and write about it.

• If you have children, try this one: When no one is around, pull the heads off a Barbie doll and a Ken doll. Stick Barbie's head on Ken and Ken's head on Barbie. Interview them about their new bodies as they sit on the sofa beside you. Write down the interview. Later, read it back to yourself and freewrite for ten minutes about what the dolls' bodies tell us about doll makers. (Reassemble the dolls quickly, before the children come home!)

• Write a poem with the following title: "How to Be A Man/ Woman."

• Try writing for ten minutes in the mind of a woman who is having an argument with a man. Stop. Write for ten minutes in the mind of the man.

• Draw a line down the center of a piece of paper. At the top of one side write *masculine* and on the other side write *feminine*. List the traits of each sex. Circle the similarities and write about them for ten minutes.

• Create a third sex using what you know of the first two. Write about it and make it come alive.

• Create a situation where a man or a woman from another era is placed in a situation that is totally incompatible with his or her view of gender. For example: A late twentieth-century feminist woman gets caught in a time warp and ends up a character in a Gothic Romance novel. Your character is supposed to be helplessly in love with the abusive co-dependent, Count Richmond. What happens?

Husbands Not Fathers / Wives Not Mothers

Now that we've played with society's gender masks it's time to look at our own personal models and how they have impacted our lives. In his book *Getting the Love You Want* (Henry Holt, 1988) psychologist Harville Hendrix talks about the dangers of the *unconscious marriage*, in which partners project childhood needs onto each other instead of standing back and exploring the new possibilities. Hendrix calls a *conscious marriage* the ability to see the contexts from which our feelings have emerged and create new contexts for ourselves.

Here's a writing exercise that begins this process. List ten qualities that either you or your spouse possess. If you are not married, list qualities you would like your spouse to possess. On another piece of paper, write ten qualities that your parent of the opposite sex possessed. Compare the two lists. Look for differences. Look for similarities. Freewrite for ten minutes about what you find.

Digging Deeper

What are the similarities between the lists? What are the major differences? How is your partner the parent you never had? What needs did you have as a child that were not met?

Opposites Attract

Last summer my wife made curtains for our bedroom. My mother was visiting and my wife told her she had measured the window exactly but the curtains still came up short. "That's what happens when you try to be too exact," my mother replied. My wife and I laughed because it seemed to typify an ongoing argument between us. I'm the sloppy estimator who has trouble doing anything to completion, let alone perfection. She is the perfectionist who uses the Scotch-Brite pad to clean the sides of each fork tine. I am the quantity person and she is the self-appointed quality control.

Why did I marry a woman who is so unlike my mother? A woman who can cut a straight line with an exacto knife. Why didn't I marry a woman who is more like me?

Sometimes I think these thoughts, especially when I watch her empty the dish drainer back into the sink because all the dishes that I washed are still dirty.

It would be so much easier if she were more like me, and yet, so much more boring. She sees things that I don't. I see things that she doesn't. The same things that torment us about each other also delight us. Sometimes I think successful marriages are like successful comedy teams, like Laurel and Hardy. Constant irritation, caused by these irreconcilable differences, can create an enjoyable tension between couples. In other words, the same irreconcilable differences that make people divorce each other are what can hold them together.

I've developed a stock line that I say to my wife whenever she becomes too fed up with my slovenly approach to life. Like all the best lines, it's simple and causes the listener to be self-reflective. I also know it's good because she has used it back on me. Here's how it goes: "If only I were just like you."

Triggers

• Make a list of the qualities that bug you about your spouse or significant other. Now imagine you are that person. Make a list of your qualities that bug that person. Freewrite for ten minutes comparing the two lists.

• Take turns pretending you are each of your parents. Make a list of what bugs them about each other. Compare it to the list from the previous trigger. Freewrite for ten minutes.

• Cavewrite a typical argument between your spouse and yourself. Make sure to include some of the key bits of dialogue like, "You can't be sorry enough."

• Pretend you are a biographer of a famous person who happens to be you. Describe your marriage through the biographer's eyes. For example:

> In the winter of 1987 Lane married a woman named Carol-lee Worth and took her to live with him in his 8 × 42-foot trailer. The couple had no honeymoon to speak of. The day after the wedding, Lane's new bride could be seen shoveling snow on the roof of the trailer. Years passed and . . .

• Imagine you never got married (if, in fact, you are married). Where would you be right now? What would you be doing? Let yourself imagine a different life, then go back to the life you are living and compare the two. Be honest with yourself.

The Humor Molecule: Using Laughter to Shift Contexts

Men think and God laughs.
— Yiddish proverb

Now that we've explored marriage and relationships I want to show you that shifting contexts doesn't have to be serious business. Writing humor can be a wonderful way to shift contexts and get a transcendent look at the human condition. A few years ago I developed a pseudoscientific lecture on understanding the source of humor. It's called the humor molecule; it was isolated in the late twentieth century by me one night while watching Rodney Dangerfield on the "Tonight Show." Here's how it works.

As human beings we basically share two central contexts. One is vulgar, crass, dirty, smelly, mean and ruthless—the context of the animal. The other is kind, considerate, dreamlike, idealistic, clean, thoughtful and moral— the context of the noble person. The first context is the nucleus of the molecule, not because it is the most important, but because it is what links us to the animal kingdom (which doesn't laugh), or the world of messy, uncut nature. The second context is the electrons that encompass all the civilized virtues, idealistic aspirations and clean sophistication.

Humor is created when these two worlds are brought together somehow. This is what I call *comic interface*. (It's illustrated on the facing page.) So let's take a joke by Rodney Dangerfield. "I went to a tough school. Teacher asks, 'What comes after a sentence?' Kid says, 'An appeal.' " The word *sentence* provides the double meaning: one from the clean world of the English teacher, the other from the gritty world of prisons and crime. We laugh at the moment one meaning explodes into the other. Let me give you a visual example. In his movie *Bananas*, Woody Allen is running from bad guys through the streets of a South American city. He turns a corner and is faced with two images. A man fixing a flat tire and a procession of monks. He grabs the four-way lug wrench and takes his place in front of the processional as the bad guys pass by. Like the word *sentence*, a lug wrench, by virtue of its shape, provides comic interface with its counterpart in the clean world—the crucifix.

Comedy constantly reminds us of the two worlds that make up the human condition. A man in a tuxedo walking proudly down the

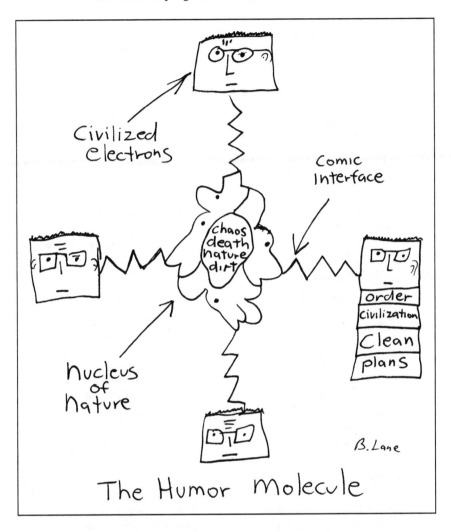

Civilized electrons

Comic Interface

chaos death nature dirt

order
civilization
Clean
plans

nucleus of nature

B. Lane

The Humor molecule

street is not funny. He is living in one world and believes he is above the rest of us. Place a banana peel on the sidewalk or, even better, a wad of dog poo and we will see a comic moment. Humor is all about awakening to the reality of life, and anybody who takes themselves seriously is a perfect target.

So far, most of my examples involve the messy world exploding the clean world but it works in the other direction too. A chimpanzee in a tuxedo is funny, as is a homeless tramp pretending to be a rich man. Charlie Chaplin proved this in his movies. The tramp's pride and undaunted insistence on being treated with dignity and respect made him funny. When we laugh at his unwillingness to accept his role as a disempowered person we acknowledge the tramp's reality. He *is* a powerful person.

Laughter is the great equalizer. It breaks down the social barriers that isolate people and unites even the most divided tribes. When we laugh we recognize ourselves and in that recognition join others. In this section I show you techniques for laughing at the oppression you unearthed in the first part of this chapter.

Flip-Flopping the World

Think of a situation where one group oppresses another group for a specific reason. Try reversing the situation by flip-flopping the original context to support the oppressed group. For example, what would a diet center be like in a society where fat was symbolic of beauty?

Digging Deeper

Is your sketch funny? Why? Was it easy to rewrite reality or was there a very loud voice in your head saying "This is silly!"? What does your piece say about the original oppression?

The Backward World

One night, when my daughter was three, she refused to put her pajamas on and go to bed. Like most parents, I was faced with a situation requiring either a stern voice or a subtle form of bribery like, "If you don't get those jammies on by the time I count to three, then no story." I am terrible at this sort of thing and my wife wasn't around to fill in. I was also exhausted. So I just threw up my hands and said, "Well, I'm from the backward world and we wear our clothes to bed and put our jammies on in the morning when we go to school." She replied, "Do you brush your teeth?" and I said, "No, our teeth brush us." That was all it took. For the next hour Jessie and I played backward world. The next day I started writing our flip-flops down. Here are a few. If you have children, try reading them a few and trying out the backward world with them.

In the backward world,
dragons save princes
from fire-breathing princesses.

In the backward world,
treasure hunts for
buried pirates.

In the backward world,
children love to clean their room
and hate to play.
Parents shout,
"Stop cleaning your room
and go outside and play right now."

In the backward world,
kittens are scary
and monsters are cuddly.

In the backward world,
all children love spinach and liver,
and their parents have to make them
eat all their ice cream.

In the backward world,
the flag says the Pledge of Allegiance to you.

In the backward world,
the puzzle puts you together.

Although at first this seems like a silly game, I've come to see it as an essential tool for gaining insight into the world. Our ability to flip-flop the world gives us distance to see the relationship between things. It helps us to gain a flexibility of mind to see solutions to problems. Try flip-flopping in your mind the next time you come across an unbearable situation. Delight in the absurdity of worlds turning over on themselves.

Triggers

- Try adding a few backward worlds to my list. Notice the silly joy of flip-flopping contexts. If you have children, play "backward world" with them. Notice how quickly they throw themselves into the joy of flip-flopping.

- Draw a cartoon of a comic moment in your life.

- Think of a time you were supposed to be sophisticated but failed. Return to that moment and write about it.

- Pretend you are a stand-up comic making laughs out of the frustrating moments of your life. Tell a few quick stories into your tape recorder. Listen to them and tell more. Let the soul of laughter work its way to the surface.

- Write a dialogue between two characters who have a secret. Make sure the secret is not revealed. Let the dialogue reflect the character's words skirting the secrets.

- Draw a cartoon of a funny moment in your life. Don't worry about your drawing skill. Revert to stick figures if you want to. Give your cartoon characters words to say.

- Write a scene for a big moment in your life. Put in the character's thoughts as subtitles. (Note: This technique was first used by Woody Allen in the movie *Annie Hall*.) For example:

> Frank: So what are you doing later tonight?
> Subtitle: Listen to me. I sound like a jerk.
> Sarah: Why do you ask?
> Subtitle: I can't believe he asked me that. I just told
> him an hour ago.

The Leap Essay

Now that we've celebrated our human ability to shift contexts through laughter its time to get a bit more serious. For the rest of this chapter we explore writing techniques that teach us to see the connections between things.

Alice Fogel, a poet and teacher formerly at the University of New Hampshire, created a form for an essay that makes the kinds of broad connections we discussed earlier. She called it the *leap essay* and defined it as any essay where you make a broad connection between one thing and another. I still remember the example she used back in 1985. Gorbachev and Reagan were meeting to discuss arms reduction at the Icelandic summit that ended in a stalemate. It was suppertime and as she listened to the news reports on the summit, she heard her dog, Emily Dickinson, barking outside. The dog's barking annoyed her. When she walked outside to punish the dog, she saw that every hair was up on the dog's back and a small cat was sitting across the driveway staring at the dog. The dog was not angry. The dog was terrified. Suddenly, it struck her that the same was true for these world leaders who spent more time barking than admitting their fear.

Firewriting

Writing leap essays is the process of jumping from the personal to the universal and back again. I've developed a technique to practice this type of thinking. It's called *firewriting* and involves letting one idea spark another. When we firewrite we jump from one event to another. We leap across time and make associations. Think of it as a more directed type of freewriting aimed at sparking analogies between the most disparate things.

Begin by stating an opinion; then compare that opinion to something else. Don't rush into it. Sit back and wait for a spark.

Here's an example of a firewrite in which I made the connection between the Elvis stamp and President Reagan.

When I look in last week's newspaper I see that Americans have overwhelmingly chosen the young Elvis over the old Elvis for the commemorative stamp. In the same newspaper is a review of a book by Patty Davis Reagan. In the new book she defines her father as a son of an alcoholic whose entire life was built around the false notion that nothing is really wrong. Americans elected Ronald Reagan because they knew they were in trouble but, like children of alcoholics, preferred to be told otherwise. That's one reason America is several trillion dollars in debt. I see a connection between these two articles. When we think of the old Elvis we think of an overweight, drug-addicted man who lived as a recluse. We think of a lonely person who, like most addicts, didn't understand or know how to take care of his own emotional needs. But the young Elvis is just a rock-and-roll idol. The pain is masked completely and he is everybody's dream of freewheelin' raw rock and roll. Americans chose Ronald Reagan for their leader. Americans overwhelmingly chose the young Elvis for their commemorative stamp. We are a country that overwhelmingly prefers the image to the reality. I remember seeing interview footage in which a star struck reporter asked the young Elvis, "Tell us. What's it like to be Elvis?" Elvis paused a minute, a little taken aback by the question. Then he shyly cocked his head and spoke almost in the voice of a little boy. "Well, there's Elvis, then there's me."

Elvis knew the difference between the image and the reality. That's more than we can say for his fans, whose chant might sound like this: "The King is dead. Long live the king!"

My firewriting draws a connection between America's fascination with Elvis and Ronald Reagan. Both men numbed themselves to the pain in their lives. I could keep going. I could suggest that a nation $3 trillion in debt is not so great at facing reality. I could talk about what it's like to be broke but to use the Visa card anyway.

When we firewrite we give ourselves permission to make wild comparisons at the risk of making little sense. Usually we find important connections and themes running through our lives.

Begin with an idea, then jump to another related idea, then jump to another related idea. Have fun when you firewrite.

Digging Deeper

Can you see strong connections between your ideas? Or, are they weak or tenuous? What do your connections tell you?

Learning to See the Connections

Peace is to earth what yeast is to bread.
— The Talmud

When I was in my twenties I shared an apartment with a college student named Jim, an unusual fellow to say the least. One day when I came home from work I found him sitting on a pillow staring at a pile of newspaper clippings covering his sky-blue floor. He had taken several newspapers and cut out all the headlines and arranged them on the floor. He told me he was studying them, looking for the connections. At the time I thought this behavior was very bizarre, even slightly psychotic; but several years later, on a plane high above the Mediterranean, I had a similar experience while reading an *International Herald Tribune*. Each headline on the front page of the newspaper seemed to be in some direct way connected to the other. The underlying principal seemed to be that the world's resources were running out and throughout the world people were struggling to keep the old battles going. The cold war was beginning to look economically unfeasible. Little did I know then that fifteen years later the connection I saw would become reality.

Learning to see the connections between things is probably the most important tool anyone can possess to prepare him or her for the twenty-first century. For hundreds of years knowledge has been the process of fragmenting thought into specialized areas. The great thinkers, the people who have changed the world, are always those individuals who are able to stand back and see the larger patterns. They are people who make new connections from old knowledge.

On the personal level our ability to see the larger patterns empowers our ability to act in new ways, discarding patterns learned to survive other contexts in our lives such as our families. As we've begun to explore, our sense of humor is directly related to our ability to stand back and see the larger patterns and to use writing as a tool for making new connections.

Triggers

• Try a *snapshot essay*. Write a leap essay composed of snapshots that may be only loosely connected. Remember a snapshot is simply a word picture of anything. Write the snapshots, then write sentences explaining the connection.

• Juxtaposing is when you place one thing beside another, usually to create a comparison. Sometimes a powerful juxtaposition can illustrate a blatant irony or hypocrisy.

For example, *Why Men Stray and Why Men Stay*, by Alexandra Penney (Bantam, 1990), tells women, "Remember that sex is your husband's greatest need." In *Out of the Shadows*, a book written for recovering sex addicts and sex offenders, psychologist Patrick Carnes writes of the core beliefs of the rapist and sexual addict: "An addict believes sex is their greatest need." This juxtaposition tells something about how conventional wisdom is synonymous with societal sickness.

Get a pair of scissors and a bunch of magazines. Try juxtaposing images and phrases that jump out at you. Delight at the connections that leap from your collage.

• Make up a *junk mail poem*. Find some junk mail and do the same thing. Look especially for words or phrases that leap out at you. Now arrange your headlines on a large sheet of white paper. Make a poem like the one on the facing page.

Meeting George McGovern

Whoever sees all beings in himself and himself in all beings does not, by virtue of such realization, hate anyone.

—Upanishads (Hindu Scriptures)

My final story about the power of shifting contexts begins at the University of New Hampshire. The 1984 New Hampshire presidential primary was in full swing and the students were once again deluged with the sound bites of would-be candidates of both parties. One man was George McGovern. He had a warm place in my heart because I voted for him in 1972 and was amazed that he was running once again. I remember ducking into the bathroom at the Student Union building and seeing a man's polished black shoes under the graffiti-strewn stall. The man was wearing a plaid suit — the same plaid suit I had seen on my favorite candidate earlier that day. I quickly remembered the men in suits standing outside the bathroom door and realized there was little doubt. The intestinal cadences coming from the stall were those of South Dakota's Senator George McGovern. Now this may sound strange, but as I stood there at the urinal I was overcome with feelings of warmth and love for George McGovern, not because he was a great liberal man who I had voted for, or that he was a fine statesman who had championed causes I believed in, or that he had decided once again, against all odds, to run for president. I was overcome with love for George McGovern because he was simply a human being like all other human beings. Why this was such a revelation, I am not sure. Looking

Junkmail

The youth bounds down the stairs and approaches the mailslot with anticipation, hoping for the letter of acceptance signaling the next step in his plans.

You have been selected to participate

Because you have an outstanding credit history, you have been pre-approved to receive one of the most sought-after charge cards around—

Remove and place one of these tokens on your Confirmation of Election to Membership and mail in the envelope provided.

Confirmation of Election to Membership

He leaves the cool haven armchair by the window, shuffles through the stench in the corridor and struggles with the mailbox lock.

Win A Year Of Unlimited Excitement.

You'll wish you were a kid again...

GREAT ADVENTURE WATCHES

For the action in your life!

She labors on a path through winter's heavy slush and darkness to the box on the roadside, a solitary woman longing for family news.

Benefit from revealing essays by distinguished fellows of The Wilson Center and other experts on events, issues, and people important to our lives today.

Dear Friend,

You may never have another chance like this one.

You surely know about "information overload." It now afflicts most literate Americans.

Bring Back the Good Times — FREE!

Junkmail....an incredible waste of energy.

back, I think it was just the uniqueness of the situation that jarred my senses.

I stood there by the urinal, reluctant to flush and risk losing this fleeting moment. I felt like I should say something, something like, "Give'm hell, George," or "I'm with you, George." But all my words seemed like public attempts to express a private feeling that had nothing to do with George McGovern. I flushed the urinal and left the bathroom before my candidate emerged from his stall.

Moments later, I stood in the foyer as George McGovern glided down the hallway in his gray plaid suit. The TV crews moved in on him as he strode along straightening his tie, brushing lint from his shoulder, smiling politely at the crowd who had gathered.

I watched him move away down the corridor trailed by a swarm of reporters and cameramen. I thought to myself about the simple biological things that make us one race—the blood, the bones, the guts of life in all of us. It was so easy to ignore our humble origins and replace them with dressed-up personalities that power us through society. Seeing George McGovern in a different context made him real to me.

When we shift contexts and see connections, the world begins to make itself known to us. In the next chapter we shift points of view to see new connections. Right now, read through your journal and look for moments where you see a new connection. Circle one such moment and freewrite about it for ten minutes. Read over your freewrite and look for more connections. Know that the process of shifting contexts and finding truth is ongoing.

In the next chapter we will reframe the world by shifting points of view. Here's one last final exercise to put us in touch with how we have shifted contexts in our own life.

Finding a Lost Friendship

Try this. Write about a lost friendship and try to discover the truth about that friendship in your writing. Remember that a lost friendship has a beginning, a middle and an end. Let your pen remember the whole friendship. Use some of these questions to probe your memory. Pay particular attention not only to how your friend changed, but how you changed and how the context of your relationship changed. Lost friendships are often caused by shifting context. For example: You met your friend in high school but then you both went to college and you drifted apart.

What attracted me to this person?
What kept the friendship going?
Was there a moment of betrayal?
When did the friendship begin to end?

Was the ending mutual?
How did this person influence you?
Why did you choose to write about this friendship and
not others?
What was the happiest moment?
What was the saddest moment?

You may want to begin with writing or make a graph of the friendship. Find the big moments and explode one. Write several snapshots of you and your friend: some from the beginning, some from the middle, and some from the end. Cavewrite the moment when your friendship ended.

Spend several weeks doing this exercise if you want. Give your pen time to remember and delight in your ability to peel back the layers and reframe the past. Tune your ears to the memories that take you by surprise and make you want to write more. Ask questions that help you to dig deeper into the heart of those memories. Find the questions you still ask yourself when you think about this person.

▪ Chapter 5 ▪

Old Stories/New Angles: Exploring Points of View

I can become you for a second and you can become me and this lifts us up.
— *Meryl Streep*

earning to see different points of view is a cognitive tool that goes hand in hand with powerful writing and critical imaginative thinking. Intelligence researcher Howard Gardner calls this type of intelligence interpersonal, or the ability to imagine the world of others. He cites it as one of the more valuable qualities children must develop to live in the twenty-first century. In the last chapter we shifted contexts and saw how this helped us to make new connections. In this chapter we imagine different points of view to achieve a deeper and broader understanding of ourselves and the world around us.

But where do we begin and what is the advantage of looking at the world from different points of view?

Broadening Vision

I took the photograph on the facing page one rainy day in London in 1979. I was standing on the sidewalk in front of Harrods department store, fascinated by the sinister-looking bald dummies in their white suits. I was also intrigued by the reflection of the building across the street in the window and how it made the dummies appear like apparitions. Just as I was about to snap the photo two people walked into the frame. They were a couple in their fifties or early sixties. The man seemed anxious and intent on going somewhere; the woman seemed bewildered and preoccupied. She was fiddling with the button on her raincoat. The man's hand was locked

in his wife's arm. He seemed unsure whether she was pulling him along or he was leading. The dummies seemed to be looking at them with some sinister intent.

A few years later I entered this photo in a contest and the judges told me it was out of focus. These judges obviously assumed the man and the wife in the foreground were the subject of the photograph. They didn't see the dummies the way I did. In their opinion that was the background of the photo. Depending on your point of view, you could say that this photograph reflects my lack of skill as a photographer or their lack of flexibility as judges. I think the "blurry" couple adds to the ghostly meaning of the photograph. Their anxiety and urgency seems so temporary and literally passing, whereas the dummies behind them have a soulful lasting quality. The dummies are in control. The people seem temporary, the dummies permanent. I could say this is a statement about a society that values things more than people.

However, I am also humble enough to see that the judges could be right. This could be just an out-of-focus photo taken by an amateur photographer of two people on a London street. Neither view is correct, but being able to see both points of view helps me to see that the photo is more than what I first imagined it to be. If I were to enter the point of view of the principal images in the photo I would learn even more ways of seeing. The dummies may be thinking of leaving the window and running up the street. The man may be thinking about this scruffy-looking man who is pretending to be Henri-Cartier Bresson. The woman may be wondering if they will make it to the theater on time. The building across the street may be reminiscing about the British Empire.

Imagining points of view frees me to discover new information and gain a broader perspective on the world. When I look at an event from the past, I am limited by the voice that speaks about that event. Throughout the first and second parts of this book we have seen how changing perception allows us to reenter our pasts with a more mature perspective. However, no matter how mature our perspective becomes, it is still limited by the boundaries of our own egos. Imagining different points of view can free us from our own perceptions and immerse us deeper into our stories.

To begin the process, we must prime our imaginations to understand other points of view. Here's an exercise I've used with many students.

Empathy Exercise: Points of View

List ten people you have disliked at any time in your life. You can include famous people but make sure you know several personally.

Pick one and list ten things that you dislike about that person. Next, pretend you are the person and list ten things that person doesn't like about you.

Look for similarities in the lists and note them. For example:

> My list:
> Tall
> Snotty
> Loud
> Always bragging

> The other person's list:
>   Short
>   Stuck up
>   Pretends not to care
>   Thinks I'm loud

Digging Deeper

Did you realize the similarities before you began this exercise?

What did you learn about yourself from the other person's point of view? What did you learn about the other person?

Hate Is a Mirror

If men were to regard the states of others as they regard their own, then who would raise up his state to attack another?

—Mo Tzu

The first time I tried out this exercise was the morning after the United States bombed Libya. I was teaching freshman composition at the University of New Hampshire and the class had a particular hate for Mohamar Ghadaffi of Libya. I had them make a list of all the qualities they disliked about him. Then I asked them to pretend they were Ghadaffi and list all the qualities they hated about President Ronald Reagan. When they compared the lists, they found similar qualities. For example, Ghadaffi was "too theatrical" and Reagan was a "movie star cowboy." Ghadaffi's view of politics was simplistic and he saw Reagan as a moron president who knew more about acting than politics. My students quickly began to move beyond their initial unexamined opinions to a deeper appreciation for the reason why these men hated each other: They were alike in so many ways.

Then we tried out the preceding exercise with people they disliked and found a similar dynamic. One student remarked that her enemy was a snob and never spoke to her. But when she entered her enemy's point of view she found that the enemy thought *she* was a snob. My student began to see what the great prophets have been teaching for centuries: Hate is a mirror. Ironically, only when my students began to see the other person's point of view did they begin to see that much of what they hate in others is also what they hate about themselves. Hate is a double-edged sword. We cannot strike out at others without suffering wounds ourselves. In the words of Buddha, "Hatred does not cease by hatred at any time, but hatred ceases by love; this is the eternal truth."

Finding many points of view helps us to see beyond our initial response to a more global understanding of the world. This is one way writing unlocks new worlds. When you look at your list of what the person you dislike thinks about you, notice the power of seeing yourself through the eyes of others.

Triggers

- If you did the exercise at the end of the previous chapter, try writing about your lost friendship from the point of view of your friend. What do you discover?
- Think of a person you really dislike. Pretend you are that person. Write in the first person describing their outlook on life.
- Think of a major confrontation in your life, with a partner, boss, child, etc. Write about it from that person's point of view using the third person.
- Get a camera and find a subject. Photograph it from many points of view. Lay the photos out on a table and pick the best one. Notice how each photo reflects different types of information.
- Retell an incident in your life from a different point of view.
- Here's a situation. Two kids are walking along and they find a ten dollar bill on the ground. Write a dialogue between them discussing what they are going to do.
- Pick two present or past world leaders who hate each other. Pretend you are each and list details about the other. Notice the similarities.
- Give a point of view to a part of your body. Write a monologue from its point of view.
For example: "A Day in the Life of a Big Toe."

Revisiting a Romance

> *It's not down on any map: True places never are.*
> *—Herman Melville*

Now that we've had some practice imagining points of view let's see how we can use them to gain a broader perspective on our own personal lives. Most of us, at one time in our life, haven't lived happily ever after; yet as children, we are often told that happily ever after is an attainable goal—whether it is the American dream or a fairy-tale romance. Looking back at old romances from new points of view can be a great way of seeing the distinction between the image of who we want people to be and the reality of who they are.

1. Begin by making a list of every romantic encounter or relationship you can remember (or want to remember). You may want to put yourself in the middle of a web chart and have your significant others orbit you. Or simply make a quick list. Don't worry if your list is incomplete. Give yourself permission to remember.

2. Pick the person from your list who you have the most unresolved feelings about. Put that person at the top of a blank page.

3. Make a list of moments you remember with this person. Include moments from the beginning of the relationship to the end.

4. Make a timeline and place the moments of the relationship along it. Start at the moment you first met your person and proceed to the moment the romance ended.

5. Pick two moments. One near the beginning of the relationship and one near the end. Freewrite for ten minutes about each moment.

6. Read over your freewrite. Now stop. Close your eyes and imagine you are the other person or simply another point of view. Write for ten minutes about each moment in this new point of view using the first person.

7. Read over your freewrites. Write one question you still have about this relationship. Freewrite an answer for ten minutes.

Digging Deeper

Was it easy to enter your ex's point of view? What new information did you learn when you told the story from that person's point of view? How has your relationship with yourself changed since you've told this story? What does your question tell you about your life since?

Cinderella Revisited

The modern world lacks not only hiding places, but certainties.
                                                    —Salman Rushdie

Finding new points of view liberates new information about our stories. If you found this exercise uncomfortable, you probably are not ready to let go of your own point of view and take another. You may feel differently in a few years. At some level, healing and self-discovery always involve forgiveness and eventually grief, but it's not always fruitful to rush the process.

Seeing the other person's point of view and asking questions frees me to see myself as a character in my past and, if I am brave enough, to really take a look at who I was. If you had trouble doing this exercise because you felt too close to the subject, the next exercise will teach you how to stand back from your life to get a clearer perspective.

Triggers

- Write the last scene of a romance novel from a different point of view. Romances are usually told from a heroine's point of view and the last scene is usually the one in which the abusive man falls into her arms.
- Pretend you are in your late nineties. Write about your first love.
- Pretend you are fourteen again. Write about love and marriage.
- Retell a happily-ever-after fairy tale, but start at the end and breathe some realism into that ending.
- Write about a first kiss.
- Do a time line of your attitude toward love. Chart the major events that caused your ideas about love to change. Pick the event that influenced you the most and write about it.
- Write your sexual autobiography. Begin with your earliest sexual memory and take yourself on a journey through the years.

The Power of Third Person

I'm about to write a novel, the only problem is I don't know if I am an I or a she.
— Elizabeth Hardwick

Along with providing new information, imagining different points of view gives us more distance from the stories we tell. Fiction writers often shift to a third-person point of view when they feel too close to their material. This is a very human thing to do and is not confined to fiction writers.

Fiction writers often create characters that embody traits in themselves or traits they wish they had. These characters give the writer a chance to explore at a distance material that is close to them.

Try this. Go back through your journal and find an event you'd like to write about. Create a character who is very much like yourself. Give the character a problem you face and write for twenty minutes. For example, you have just decided to give up smoking. Create a character who has decided to give up smoking. Put the character in a situation where there is temptation to smoke.

Digging Deeper

Did you feel close to your character? How is your character different from you? How does your character deal with the problem differently?

Lyndy Loo Stories

When my daughter Jessie Lynn was little, my wife found an effective way to help her process traumatic experiences. She would tell her *Lyndy Loo stories*. Lyndy Loo was a little blonde-haired girl about the same age as Jessie Lynn and often had the same experiences. There was the day Jessie Lynn witnessed an automobile accident and her mother left her in the car to help the victim. Lyndy Loo had a similar experience and also cried in her car seat. Jessie learned to ask for Lyndy Loo stories whenever she was upset about something.

Writing fiction in the third person has a similar effect. It frees us to explore dimensions of ourselves we have only begun to imagine. It's one way to gain distance from our lives and go deeper into issues we are not anxious to explore.

Experimenting with different points of view helps us to see the power of other perspectives. Besides third person we can write stories in second person or first person. Here are the same two sentences in the three persons.

I told her not to come but she came anyway. What was I going to do?

You told her not to come but she came anyway. What were you going to do?

He told her not to come but she came anyway. What was he going to do?

Notice the unique power of each example. Tenses can also add power. These three examples were written in the past tense. Listen to how they sound in the present tense.

I tell her not to come but she comes anyway. What can I do?

You tell her not to come but she comes anyway. What can you do?

He tells her not to come but she comes anyway. What can he do?

What would these examples sound like in the future tense? Try experimenting with points of view and tenses in your writing. Here are some triggers to get you started.

Triggers

- Think of a person you dislike. Try writing from that person's point of view in the first person for five pages. Reread what you've written and ask yourself why you dislike this person.
- Write a third-person account of a big moment in your life. Switch it to second person. Note the difference.
- Create an author who is creating a character like him- or herself.
- Write a scene in which a character must confront a serious problem. Try it in first, second or third person. Note the difference in tone.
- Create a character who is like you were twenty years ago. Begin by drawing a picture, then write a snapshot describing the picture. Pick a situation and put the character in it.
- Enter the mind of a friend or a member of your family. Put that person in a situation and write about it.
- Write about yourself in the third person. Move between your thoughts, actions and voice.
- Interview a family member about the central events of his or her life. Return to one of those events and write about the person in the third person.
- Write an opening chapter of a novel about an old woman or man looking back on life.
- Paint a landscape with a single figure standing alone. Then paint the thoughts inside that figure's head.

• Tell a Lyndy Loo story to yourself about something traumatic that happened in your life. Tape record it and listen to it before you go to bed.

• Make up a fairy tale about something that happened in your life.

• Tell a story about a moment of discovery in your life. Experiment with it in the first person, second person, then the third person. What is the difference?

Cigarettes Are Good for You: Truth Is Funny

If you can find humor in it, you can survive it.
— Bill Cosby

Just as switching points of view brings us closer to the truth in history, a satirical point of view can help us to sift reality from fantasy and gain a critical understanding of the world. Nowhere is this more evident than in the way we look at commercials.

All commercials lie to some extent. Let's face it, one product is not usually much better than another. But the worst offenders are harmful and dangerous products like cigarettes and alcohol. Some people feel this type of commercial should be outlawed; others, like myself, feel this would only solve half the problem. We need to teach people to interpret and understand the messages they are bombarded with from birth. We need to teach children to get into the habit of separating image from reality.

Taking the point of view of advertising executive for an alcohol or cigarette company can illuminate both the society we live in and what it is trying to tell us and sell us. It can also be a recipe for satire. The following exercise teaches satire and critical thinking in a way everyone can understand.

The Image and the Reality

A joke is total knowledge in a nanosecond.
— Steve Martin

Here is an exercise I've used with great success in high school to teach a truthful satirical point of view and have a great time.

Pick a drug like cigarettes or alcohol. Make a list of all the nasty effects of the drug. For example:

Alcohol
> Makes you dizzy
> You say things you don't mean
> You get violent
> You throw up
> You smash your car
> You beat a family member

Once you have your list, imagine you are an advertising executive with a problem. Your product has all these negative properties, but you nevertheless have to find a way to sell it to people. You must invent an image about your product and promote it with that image. Consult liquor and beer ads for ideas. Give your product a name that goes along with the image but somehow includes the reality.

For example:
> Smash: The beer of race driving champions.
> Passion: The drink for lovers.

Write a commercial that promotes your image but that also includes the negative reality of the drug you are trying to promote. This is the one thing that will distinguish your commercial from those on television. It also should make your commercial funny. If you have access to a video camera, record your commercial and see if you can run it on the local cable station.

Digging Deeper

Is your commercial funny? Why or why not? How does the reality reflect on the image?

Dressing Up as the Enemy

A satirical point of view often elucidates the truth about the thing it is satirizing. Satirists often dress up as the enemy, take in their audience and then gradually reveal their true cards.

A classic example of this is Jonathan Swift's famous essay, "A Modest Proposal." At the time it was written many English planners were publishing essays on the problem of Ireland. This impoverished, oppressed country, which England happened to have invaded, was now a British problem. Swift begins his essay mimicking these English planners and their mechanistic tone of voice. By the end of the essay we discover his plan is to feed the Irish families by having them eat their own babies. One can imagine the impending horror of those men who began to read this essay nodding their heads in earnest. The goal of satire is not only to criticize, but to make people conscious of the deficiencies in a particular point of view.

Triggers

- Try satirizing one of the following voices:
  A network newsperson
  An insurance salesperson
  A doctor
  A narrator on a commercial

- Satirize a voice from your personal childhood. For example: "Eat your string beans, children in India are starving."

- Watch TV for an hour looking for images of women or men from the commercials. Find one and write about it for ten minutes in his or her voice.

- Get some perfumey magazines like *Cosmopolitan, GQ* or *Vogue*. Find several images of men and women from ads. Hang them up on the wall above your writing area. Write a dialogue between these characters. Have them speak what is in their soul, not just what is in their organs.

- Cut out images of people from magazines and paste them on a big blank sheet of paper. Give your images names like, "Glamour Guy," "Sultry Sam," etc. Write a dialogue between them.

- Go through a magazine with a stack of Post-Its. Write the real message under the image of each ad. For example, on a beer ad showing a football player going up for a pass in front of a bottle of the product, the message is, "This beer will make you a better football player." Notice how the real message is often a lie.

Creating Satirical Voices

Find a voice that bugs you; a voice that makes your life harder to live; a voice that lies to you. It could be your Aunt Margaret's voice, the voice of the computer in your car, the voice of the sweepstakes letters you receive in the mail, or the voice of a man or woman on a TV commercial. Write in this voice for ten minutes. Don't worry so much about content, just let the voice speak and see what it says. Then stop, stand back from the voice and look at it. Ask yourself this question: Why does this voice bug me so much? When you have answered this question, write for another ten minutes trying to exaggerate the qualities in the voice that bug you.

Digging Deeper

What did it feel like to write in the voice? What does your exaggeration say about the original voice?

Total Literacy by the Year 2000

When I read the memo I was mad, hopping mad. It was written by the leader of a literacy board and spoke in a very snooty tone about the need for total literacy by the year 2000. As a teacher who has worked in adult literacy I was appalled by the lack of sensitivity. We are all learning to be better readers and writers. To assume that some people can read and write and others can't is to condemn the illiterates until they can be magically enlightened.

Furthermore, literacy was viewed by this man as a means to cultural superiority rather than as a tool for empowering writing and thinking. In the past I have written letters to the editor on this same issue. I have pointed out the fact that headlines like "Local Libraries Battle Illiteracy" talk about underprivileged people as though they were infected by some plague.

Rather than write another letter to the editor I decided to try a sneakier approach. I called my essay, "Total Literacy by the Year 2000 *Is* Attainable," and just like you did in the previous exercise, I began by mimicking the voice of cultural superiority that disturbed me in the original memo. I spoke of the memo as an important document and heartily agreed with its author. I spoke of the unenlightened masses who remain chained to their TV sets unable to participate in the world of great literature. Several paragraphs later, however, I laid all my cards on the table. Here is my plan for total literacy by the year 2000. Notice how much fun I had mimicking and magnifying the unconscious attitudes toward literacy that disturbed me.

A Modest Proposal for a Completely Literate Vermont

1. No Talking: The tenaciously illiterate cultures of the world all share what is naively labeled "oral culture." These unfortunate civilizations—such as native Americans, Australian Aborigines and Bushman of the Kalihari—have existed for thousands of years without a written language. If one had to point out a single cultural practice that allowed this disturbing condition to persist generation upon generation, speaking would be the culprit. Though the sacrifice of oral communication may prove discomforting for literate Vermonters and require a state investment in many pads and pens, a law forbidding speech would inexorably force the illiterates of Vermont to surrender themselves to enrollment in adult education programs.

2. Literacy Checkpoints: Since the State Department of Education and other affiliated state agencies have enlisted in the battle against illiteracy, should not the Vermont State Police, hithertofore required to spend so much of their time aggravating intoxicated drivers—some of whom are highly literate people—should not these stalwart enforcers of public approbrium lend their specialized efforts to this noble cause? Imagine, if you will, these brave women and men shouldering their part in this historic endeavor. You are driving down Interstate 89. You notice a road block ahead. The state trooper leans over as you roll down your window. "Complete this quote," she says. "Tomorrow and tomorrow and tomorrow leaps in its petty pace from day to day to the last syllable of recorded time." In a flash, your mind leaps to complete the soliloquy: "And all our yesterdays have lighted fools the way to dusty death." You respond, softly weeping with the pathos and beauty of the moment. You and the trooper lock eyes, a literate's embrace, smile pensively and go your separate, yet more ennobled, ways. If, however, you stare blankly in an uncomprehending daze, prepared to respond with only your immediate mental obsession—"Huggies, Cheerios, Similac?"—you will be enrolled in a mandatory Shakespeare program. Though your driver's license will not be revoked on a first offense, your literacy probation period will last a year, at the end of which time you will be expected to have familiarized yourself with Greek Tragedy or to read all children's books that have received Newbury Awards or Caldecott medals. In addition, an essay test will be given.

If you are stopped at a literacy checkpoint and it is proven that, besides being ignorant of Shakespeare, you cannot read, your vehicle will be seized and you will be taken immediately to a Shock Literacy Boot Camp located somewhere near Derby Line. There you will be incarcerated for several weeks in a small cell with a speaker in the ceiling playing excerpts from *Hooked on Phonics* twenty-four hours a day.

3. The Price of Total Literacy: Finally, as we pursue our heroic goal of total literacy for Vermonters by the year 2000, there is one unfortunate problem that cannot be alleviated through these simple guidelines. Research has proven that certain special people, will never, in Mr. _____ 's words, "join an adult citizenry made up of people who love reading and who pass on the love of books." This great human tragedy affects thousands of Vermonters who suffer from congenital hearing loss, mental retardation and other learning disabilities. It is with great concern for the collective well-being of literate Vermonters that I recommend that all these unfortunate souls be relocated in another state which demands a less stringent standard of literacy. New Jersey or Texas are two states that come to mind, though some have suggested one-way Greyhound specials from Burlington to the West Coast—a local tradition. Though this necessity seems somewhat severe, we must realize that our goal of *total* literacy by the year 2000 does not permit us to be soft on individual illiteracy.

I hope as you study this simple three-point plan you will see that it is in keeping with the goals of the Literacy Council. I hope that you, gentle reader, are one of the thousands of Vermonters ready to raise arms against the scourge of illiteracy that has infected Vermont far too long and has now reached epidemic proportions. And if you are one of the 60,000 unfortunate souls who cannot decipher this essay, remember that as long as there are well-meaning, inspired, literate people like myself ready and willing to sacrifice their all for your sake, you must never relinquish your secret heart's hope of reading the *Odyssey*.

Triggers

• You are an alien from the planet Centaur, where people are asexual. Describe human beings' courtship rituals in a letter home.

• Pretend trees are the most advanced of all creatures. Take a tree's point of view and describe the peculiar animal species known as human beings.

• Try this one with your spouse or intimate friend. What does it mean to be taken care of? Make a list of your needs. Have the other person make a list of his or her needs. Compare lists and discuss ways of meeting them.

• Write a manual for new babies written from an experienced toddler's point of view.

• Write from the point of view of an oppressed food or animal.

Here's Vermont poet Geof Hewitt's poem about an empowered turkey.

Lightning Turkey
I am a lightning turkey,
so named because I run and run,
run so fast the bullet can't catch up,
run so fast the grass beneath my feet catches fire.
I am a lightning turkey
the color of the wind and built for speed.
Built for speed so Thanksgiving doesn't faze me,
built for speed because I am always the day after
    Christmas,
built for speed for I am the whizzing wonder of the
    whole green earth,
built for speed because my drums are for beating,
not eating, not cooking, not plucking, not stuffing,

> not saying a prayer over and calling it grace,
> not washing me down with champagne,
> not picking me apart the days after the holidays,
> nor slicing me into sandwiches with lots of mayonnaise.
> For I am a lightning turkey. My song will waken the
>   world,
> my scream will boil the blood of pilgrims,
> my life will be an example.
> For I shall be the president of all turkeys,
> and from their bones, reconstruct the flesh
> and put the guts back in from before they were
>   dressed
> and stick each feather back into its feather hole,
> replace the heads and beaks, the tongues and wattles,
> and set them fluttering back in life's barnyard,
> endowed with my speed, my appetite for man.

Dream Points of View

Just as finding satirical points of view gives us control over oppressive situations and shows us a broader, humorous perspective in our conscious lives, finding new points of view can also help us to get a clearer picture of our dreams. This exercise, based on Fritz Perls's Gestalt therapy, can help put you in touch with the larger implications of your dreams.

Begin by keeping a dream journal for a few weeks. Write down dreams as soon as you wake up. Don't worry about not remembering your dreams; just start writing whatever fragments you may remember. If you're like me, you'll find that the process of writing helps you to remember.

When you have a dream you want to work with, make a list of all the points of view in the dream. A point of view can be a person or an object in the dream. Let your imagination have fun with this exercise.

Pick three points of view and freewrite for ten minutes from each.

Digging Deeper

Were you surprised by information or feelings brought up by any point of view? What new information did you learn about the dream? Which point of view was the most revealing?

The Gestalt of Life

Psychologist Fritz Perls, like his teacher Sigmund Freud, believed that all images in dreams were alienated parts of ourselves. The exact meaning of these parts is a subject of debate. Therapy involved giving a voice to all these fragmented selves and hearing what they had to say. Only when all the voices were out did we begin to see the whole or what Perls labeled the Gestalt. According to Perls, seeing life from all the different points of view was key to being healthy. I think you'll see the truth of Perls's idea by the end of this chapter.

Years ago I took a psychology class at the University of New Hampshire in which we interpreted our dreams through Perls's theory. Each of us would role play the people and symbols in our dreams. I had a dream that my brother and I were children and we were walking with my father on the old railroad bridge over the Cocheco River in Dover, New Hampshire. A train was coming and I climbed under the bridge and clung to the rafters as the train went over. As I hung on, I wondered what happened to my brother and father. Then I woke up.

When I acted out this dream I first took the point of view of my brother and father.

Michael and Daddy: There's nothing to worry about, the train won't hurt us.

Then I took my point of view.

Me: Are you crazy? That train is heading straight toward us. Let's get out of here!

Then I took the train's point of view. Suddenly I knew what the dream was about.

Train: I'm gonna get you. Run as fast as you can. Run as far as you can. I'm gonna get you. You can't escape me!

The train was reality, or Death—the common denominator. When I acted it out for the class I could feel my heart pounding faster and my voice grow deep and raspy. I could feel the urgency and power. I was shaking by the time I was through.

Acting out the dream helped me to see that my brother and father are the part of me that avoids, that pretends nothing's wrong.

(I was very casual and calm and a little spacy sounding when I acted out their voices.)

This ties in with my core story where I'm always trying to separate the reality from the fantasy. My brother and father don't make the distinction. They fantasize no danger and expect me to believe it. But I see the train coming. I'm the one who looks for reality; I hid. But this makes me alone, in the dream, under the rafters of the bridge.

Looking at points of view in this dream helps me to analyze and see my core story better. The next exercise applies the same idea to our conscious lives.

Triggers

• Keep a dream journal for a month. Keep it near your bed with a flashlight. Write down your dreams, even fragments, as soon as you wake up. The more you write them, the more you remember. When you have a dream you want to explore, try giving each of its elements and people a voice. Write your dreams like a play.

• Cavewrite a dream. Draw pictures of the major players and give a voice to their thoughts and feelings. What themes emerge?

• Write a dialogue between images in a dream.

• Return to a dream that intrigues you. Pretend you have gone on vacation into your dream. Send a postcard back to yourself.

• Create a dream that illustrates an anxiety you've had lately.

• Create a dream that reflects your own personal peace of mind. Cavewrite it first or dive right in.

The Three Faces of Me: Schizophrenia Made Simple

I seek strength, not to be greater than my brother, but to fight my greatest enemy, myself.

—From a Native American prayer

Imagine for a moment that there are distinct characters living inside you. You are like a schizophrenic person from some old movie like the *Three Faces of Eve*. One of these personalities might be a joker, the other a serious person, the third a child. Cavewrite a picture of these personalities. Add as much detail as possible and give them something to say.

Once you've established the three characters, write a dialogue between them.

Digging Deeper

What is the relationship between the three personalities? Is any one person the boss? Which person do you like the best? Which do you like the least?

The Cast

When I split up my personality I find three basic parts: a worrier, a jester and a smiler. Here is a typical dialogue between them.

> Worrier: Come on. Let's get going. We'll be late.
>
> Jester: Late, late. We're always late. Who cares?
>
> Smiler: Smell the roses, chill out; take it easy.
>
> Worrier: You're wasting time when you should be working. Get going.
>
> Smiler: What does it mean to waste time? Stay happy. Live now.
>
> Jester: Time is where the clock is.

Splitting my personality helps me to delight and cringe and see different aspects of myself. It also helps me to see which voices make me happy when they are in control and which make me miserable. My worrier is a torment in my life. He always wants to be someplace different. He is never content. When he is in control there is no peace. My smiler is a joy. Though he has no ambition, he is grateful and enjoys each moment. My jester is a delight to me because he is always playing with my sense of reality to give me a laugh. When he is in control, life is chaotic and unstructured but loads of fun.

Which of your personalities would you prefer to be in control? List a few positive and negative traits of each.

Triggers

• Split your mother's or father's personality three ways. Draw pictures of the three. Cavewrite a moment or write a short poem from each personality's point of view.

• Create a situation where your three personalities must reason together. For example: They are stuck in an elevator. Write a dialogue between the three.

- Go back to a moment in your life when you had to make an important decision. Create three personalities that made their voices known to you at the time.
- Split the personality of a public figure like the president or a movie star.
- Split the personality of an animal. (Cats work particularly well.) Draw pictures of each personality and show how they speak to each other in a particular situation.

Splitting Stories

So far in this chapter we have learned to imagine different points of view. We have played with the third person and learned that experimenting with points of view can bring healing laughter as well as a heightened vision of the world. Now, it's time to apply some of this knowledge to our core stories. Find a story from your journal. A story you enjoy telling.

Mapping Points of View

Look back through your stories in your journal. Find one that you'd like to explore further. Pick a story that has some emotional conflict, a story that is unresolved. If you can't find a story, use a dream that you've had recently. Make a web of all the points of view in your story as I've done on the facing page. A point of view can be that of a person, a tree, the wind, a parking meter or anything else in the story. Instead of a web you may want to list the points of view in the story.

Pick one unusual point of view and write for twenty minutes.

Digging Deeper

What did you learn when you entered the new point of view? How does this new knowledge change your original perception of the story? Is there any other point of view that wants to be written from?

Mrs. Carberry's Point of View

I decided to go into Mrs. Carberry's point of view. She was the kindergarten teacher who shook me in Chapter 2. I asked myself what she was thinking and this is what I came up with.

"What's wrong with this child? Why doesn't he know

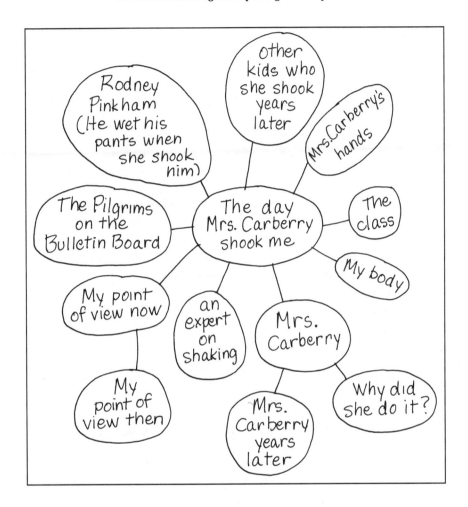

the answer? Perhaps I am not a good teacher? No, it's him. Look at him. He doesn't pay enough attention. And he was absent for a week or two. Sure. He probably told his mother I was an old battle-axe. He's got the answer in there. I'll get it. I'll shake it out of him. That's what I'll do. I won't let him say that I'm not a good teacher. It's not my fault he wasn't paying attention. I'll show him. Spacy child."

By entering Mrs. Carberry's point of view I learn that she was not just a mean woman. She was a victim of an educational system that created an oppressive model of correctness. She shook me to make up for her own sense of inadequacy as a teacher and her despair. This does not mean what she did to me was excusable. However, seeing her point of view helps me to forgive her. And as a person, I can't move on until I can forgive her.

I spend a great deal of time traveling around the country helping teachers to teach writing in a way that does justice to the individual voices of their students. Many teachers, in following the precepts of the Whole Language movement, have learned to give up their absolute authority in the classroom and to encourage individual choice and expression among their classes. I give ideas and techniques for nurturing and instructing these teachers.

Every so often in my travels, I think of Mrs. Carberry shaking me so I'd get the right answer. And now, after doing this exercise, I will tell teachers about how my fear of Mrs. Carberry was in reality a fear that she passed on to me from her teachers. You see, she never got the right answer either and that's why she shook me. I learned this through thinking and writing, from both my own and her point of view and from writing this book. I know something now that Mrs. Carberry didn't know: There is no right answer, only more questions that we can shake gently out of ourselves.

Triggers

• Find an inanimate point of view, like that of a table, chair or hat and retell the same story.

• Split your personality into three parts the way we did in an earlier exercise. Give your three persons names that correspond with your reality at that moment. Use names like Heart, Mind, Emotions. Write a dialogue between all three at the time of the story.

• Return to your childhood and retell a story to your own child within. As it unfolds, explain to your child exactly what is happening with your adult voice. Comfort your child in your writing; tell her how much you love her. Explain the situation and tell your child that understanding will come with time but that she has a right to feel that way.

• Buy or make a pie. Slice the pie into as many points of view as you want. Label the pieces with Post-Its. Pull out the points of view you wish to explore. Freewrite for ten minutes. Then eat the pie. Repeat until all the pie is eaten. (Note: This exercise works better with more than one person for digestive reasons.)

• Take a roll of photos of a subject. Notice how each photo freezes an aspect of the subject's personality. Pick three photos and give each a voice.

• Write from the point of view of a person you idolized. Have the person explain a personal weakness.

Reentering the Picture

Now that we've played with and imagined many points of view, we are ready to reenter old memories and learn to intervene on the voices in our head with the new knowledge that playing with points of view has given us. Only then do we gain the power to reimagine our lives and the world we live in.

In the next part, we begin mapping how stories change in the retelling. In Chapter 7 we learn how to intervene on those stories with new voices and ideas. In the final chapter, we practice imagining ourselves and our world anew. For now, take a break and look over your writing. Delight in all the different aspects of your personality that shine through in different places. Know that there is no one else on the planet quite like you. If you want to take a break, try the following excercise.

Masking Reality

Invite a friend over and borrow or buy a book like Carole Sivan's *Maskmaking* (Worcester, Mass: Davis Publications Inc., 1986). Take turns making plaster masks of each other's faces. Paint and decorate your finished mask with whatever you can find. Don't think about it too much, just do it. When it's all done, lay it on the floor and look at it. Talk about your mask and what it means to you. Give your mask a voice. Put it on and become it for a minute or two. Feel its breath inside you. Love it. Give it a voice. Write in that voice for ten minutes. Know all the powers and points of view inside you waiting to be noticed. Understand your uniqueness and cherish it. Hang your mask on the wall near your writing desk.

Part Three

Reexperiencing

There must come a time . . . all your mirrors turn to windows.
— *Pamela Frankau*

▪ Chapter 6 ▪

Recycling Stories:
The Dance of Words and Meaning

> I will tell you something about stories,
>   (he said).
> They aren't just entertainment.
>   Don't be fooled.
> They are all we have, you see,
>   all we have to fight off illness and death.
>
> —Leslie Silko

In the last two chapters you learned to reflect and search for new patterns and truth in your stories. In this final section of the book we examine the process of telling and retelling the same core stories differently at various times in our life and reexperiencing and reimagining those experiences with new eyes.

In this chapter we search for ways of mapping the progress of a story through time. I call this *story cycles* to accentuate the circular nature of retelling stories. Understanding story cycles will help us to begin the process of gaining distance from our core stories. Ultimately, this distance will allow us the power to reimagine ourselves and the world we live in. We focus on this imaginative power in Chapters 7 and 8.

Finding the Story's Voice

> An artist must shut up when his work begins to speak.
> —Friedrich Nietzsche

Every story has a voice that speaks to the teller whenever they tell it. Listening and examining the tone of that voice can help us find the truth of the story.

Think of a story you have told at different times in your life. Perhaps it is a story from your childhood or maybe your adulthood. It's a story that you have told many times. Now pretend the story is a person with a voice that tells you valuable information. What did it tell you at the time the story occurred? What does the story tell you now? Give the story a voice and let it talk to you directly. Freewrite for ten minutes answering these two questions.

Digging Deeper

How has the voice of the story changed? How has it stayed the same? What has influenced this change the most?

The Story of Pinky

If we assume that all stories are an attempt to tell the truth, then looking at how we told stories at different periods of our lives to different audiences gives us a portrait of our ability to perceive truth at any given time.

Sarah found this out through the story of Pinky, one of her earliest childhood memories. She was two years old at the time and her dearest loved toy was a teddy bear named Pinky. The family was living in an apartment in New York City and Sarah's mother was going through a very stressful period in her life. One night Sarah's mother was mad at her for not cleaning her room. In order to get Sarah motivated, she threatened to throw Pinky down the incinerator slot in the hallway. Sarah was horrified by her mother's threat and found herself telling this story to friends her whole life.

When she examined the way she told the story to herself back then, the voice of the story sounded like this: "You are a sloppy person. Being sloppy can be dangerous to your toys. Don't be sloppy. Don't be who you are."

Years later, Sarah often laughed when she told this story to friends. When she wrote down the voice of that later story, it sounded like this, "Your childhood was the pits. How helpless you were as a little girl. You were so alone with that woman's anxiety. You should be angry about this. Why does it seem so funny now?"

Each voice tells Sarah as much about her story as about herself. Her earlier story blames herself. Her later version begins to see her mother's role more clearly. Listening to the voice of a story at different times in our lives and with different audiences frees us to see beyond old conceptions of what the story means to a more recent understanding of who we are. In the next exercise we explore how an awareness of the audience can help us get closer to the meaning of our core stories.

Triggers

• Retell your mother's or father's stories. Change them in some way to accent what you hear in them.

• Retell stories about yourself told by parents, siblings and friends.

• Retell the story of your own life starting at the present and working backward.

• Follow this lead: "I never knew the real story about _____ till now. . . ."

The Power of Audience

As we saw in the last exercise, often the voice of our stories is interconnected with the individual we tell the story to. In this exercise we explore the influence of audience on how our stories speak to us.

List all the people you remember telling the story to and the approximate year when you told the story.

Now pick two people from your list. Try to remember when you told them the story and how it felt afterward. Imagine you are telling them your story. When you get to the end, write down the feeling you had when you finished.

Digging Deeper

How does the story change with the different audience? Which audience makes you feel the most comfortable? Which helps you to understand the real story?

Pinky's Revenge

"That was a sadistic thing to say," the psychologist said to Sarah, who was thirty-eight years old and being treated for depression.

That was the moment Sarah's Pinky story cycle ended. She cried as she sat there in the sunny office. The psychologist was right. It was a sadistic thing to say. But nobody, in all the years she told the story, ever said it. Her mother's behavior was seen as irrational or even crazy. She had a bad temper. But nobody had ever recognized the sadistic nature of a thirty-year-old woman threatening to destroy a two-year-old's teddy bear — nobody until now. Hearing those words helped Sarah, after years of telling and retelling her Pinky story, to finally let go of it. "I don't have to tell the Pinky story any more," Sarah said when I interviewed her.

The right audience can be the perfect catalyst to ending a story cycle.

Triggers

• Tell the same story to two friends. Pay close attention to your feeling about the story as you tell it. Freewrite for ten minutes about the difference of telling the story to each friend. Answer this question: Which friend brings you closer to the truth of the story?

• Tape-record a story imagining you're a radio talk show host broadcasting to the entire world. Wait a few days, then listen to the broadcast. Write a fan letter to yourself and tell how you identified with the story. Provide insight into the talk show host's character.

• Explain an adult story in a way that a young child can understand it.

• Tell a story about something that happened to you as an adult. But tell it in a letter to the child inside you. Begin with "Dear Child."

• Pretend you are a historian from the year 2310. You are presenting a paper on the lives of common Americans in the latter twentieth century. Write about your life exemplifying any point you choose.

Making a Story Wheel

If we could graph the process of recycling stories, what would it look like? I've designed my own model to illustrate this dynamic process. It's called a *story wheel* and it's a tool for generating questions about our stories told through time.

Make several enlarged photocopies of the blank diagram on page 128 or simply copy it onto a blank page in your journal. Follow these steps and fill in the blanks. See what happens.

1. In the three sections, write down three distinct times you told your story to different audiences, or three separate stories with a similar theme.

2. Write down the voice of the story for each of the three versions.

3. When you hear the voice of the story, what feelings arise in you? Write feelings from back then on the left side and feelings now on the right side.

4. Look at what you've written in your story wheel and imagine for a moment that the wheel is beginning to spin. As the wheel spins, questions will spin off each of the three sections; these are questions that would ordinarily be trapped inside. Write down these questions on the outer rim of the story or outside the diagram.

5. Pick the most intriguing question and freewrite for ten minutes.

Digging Deeper

How do the questions differ from one story to the next or one telling to the next? Did anything in your story wheel surprise you? How did the voice of the story change?

Why Did You Do That to Me?

Here's Sarah's story wheel (page 129). Notice how the early versions of her story blame herself and the later versions blame her mother. Only the final story begins to see both her mother and herself in perspective.

But more importantly, notice how her early questions are about her own inadequacy, whereas her later questions are about trying to understand her mother's behavior and her own anger at that behavior. As the story wheel spins through the years, larger truths emerge. As we explore and question those truths, we begin to get a clearer picture of who we are today.

Truth comes in circles. Recently I saw Kevin Locke, a Lakota Sioux man, lecture on this subject. He said he found great difficulty explaining what a circle truly is to American schoolchildren. He said that when the Europeans first came to America the Lakota had a word for them that translated as "the people who make things square." He offered, "How can I explain to them what a circle is when they live in square rooms? When they are thirsty they go to the square kitchen and walk to the square refrigerator and take out

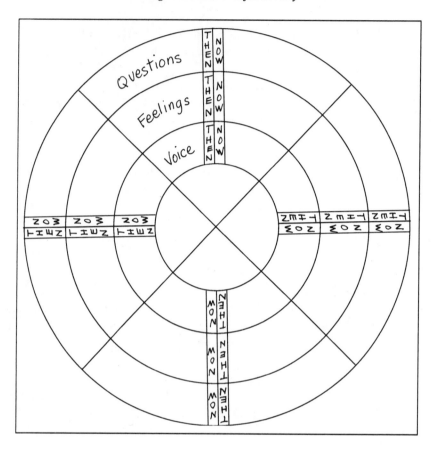

the square carton of milk. When I fly in a plane I look down and see the square fields."

It is no wonder we are accustomed to thinking in a linear manner. We grow frustrated when life teaches us the same lesson we thought we learned earlier. We get discouraged because we don't accept that life is circular. But once we acknowledge the circular pattern of life, we begin to take part in it. We see connections that seemed like obstructions before. We live in harmony with our stories. They grow like great trees around us. Look at your story wheel. Look for glimpses of truth in how the voice and questions of your stories change.

Triggers

- Make a story wheel with three core stories about the same

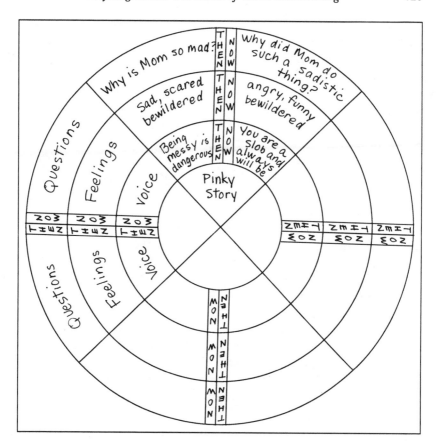

theme instead of three retellings. Explore the interconnecting voices of your stories and the questions that emerge from them.

• Get a red and a blue colored pencil. Shade in the outer rim of the story circle with red. This color represents unresolved questions. Purple represents resolved questions. Shade over the red with blue to make purple in the sections that are more resolved. Hang your story wheel on your wall near your writing desk. Pin it in the center and give it a spin when you are looking for something to write about.

• Make a story wheel of three family stories. Pick the questions that intrigue you the most and write about them.

• Invent your own model to illustrate the progress of stories. Share it with a friend or send it to me in care of my publisher.

Family Core Stories

Now that we've begun to see how story cycles work, we can look at our family's core stories and study how we and others tell and retell them.

Here's how to start. Write down *Family Stories* in the middle of a blank sheet of paper. Web stories your parents and grandparents told you. Pick one that intrigues you and freewrite about it for ten minutes. Reread the story and write down five questions about it. Pick one question and write for another five minutes.

Find the big moment in the story and explode it on another page in your journal.

Digging Deeper

Why did you pick this story? Did you learn anything about the original story from answering your question? What similarities exist between the stories? What do they tell you about the teller?

Recycling Family Stories

My father had a dog named Pal. He fed it leftover ice cream from the Breyer's ice cream factory. He was a scruffy little mutt with one ear up and the other down. Like my father, he lived on the streets of Brooklyn and they took an immediate shine to each other. My father's voice grew heavy with emotion whenever he described Pal. "We were like brothers," he would say. "Everywhere I would go, he would go. Then one day, Pal ran away. Or someone took him. I don't know. All I know is he was gone. I spent days searching for him, up and down the streets and alleys of Brooklyn. But no luck. Months pass and I'd totally given up hope of finding him. I was with my friends in the street playing stickball. Who should show up? Pal. He's skinny and sick looking. He's hopping on three legs and his mouth is all foamy like a beard hanging from his chin. That's how dogs get when they have rabies or distemper or some other bad disease. But what do I know? I'm a kid. He's my dog. My brother. He comes up to me and his mangy tail wags. He lays down on the sidewalk right in front of me and asks me to rub his belly. I know he's real sick because he doesn't move when I throw the ball and say, "Come on boy. Go get it."

Pal died the next day and his story ended with him, or so I

thought until just right now as I sit here writing. As I wrote about Pal I got to thinking of my own first dog, Snoopy. Snoopy was a young puppy barely a year old when he ran away for three days. I was devastated. I loved that dog like only a twelve-year-old boy can love a dog. I couldn't sleep and refused to eat for the first day, and I remember my father telling me he would come back. He was sure of it. My father had been working late that week, and when he got home the first thing he'd ask was, "Is Snoopy back?"

On the third day, just before dusk, Snoopy returned wagging his tail with the unrestrained pride of an unfixed male dog. He was glad to be home and I was more than delighted to see him, but my father didn't get home until late. When he saw Snoopy I heard him say, "Thank God."

"Where have you been?" my mother had asked him. She had called work and found he had left at the normal time. He told us he had been looking for the dog all week, driving from town to town, searching alleyways and parking lots. Each night he had chosen a different place to search. He knew Snoopy was alive but he wasn't sure he would ever find him. I remember feeling so happy that Snoopy was back. I also remember feeling such a great love for my father because he had tried so hard to find him for me. But as I write this I'm thinking that my father had another mission besides assuaging the grief of his twelve-year-old son. He was reliving his own story and was determined to have a different outcome this time.

Snoopy wasn't really sick. But I could tell he hadn't eaten for days from the wild look in his eyes that dogs get when they have their own stories to tell. The dog lived for many years after I left home and he became my father's best friend—always at his side, the recipient of many a dinner scrap.

As I write this I think of my father strolling the back alleys in the next world. Two mutts tag along behind him, sniffing his footsteps.

Triggers

• Make a story wheel using three family stories. Try to answer the most intriguing question that flies off the wheel.

  • Tell a family story from two different points of view.

  • Cavewrite the big moment in a family story. Include several questions in your cavewrite that get to the heart of the moment.

• Interview your oldest living relative. Tape-record the stories. Pick one and paint a picture that gets to the heart of the story.

• Pick a theme like getting lost or running away. Ask your mother and father for stories about the theme. Write their stories down and then write some of your own. Compare the stories or make story wheels.

The Old Stories: Core Stories From the Past

Studying family stories can help us to see connections from one generation to the other. Old stories have been recycled for many generations. They tell us about our culture and give us a chance to resee where we came from. Here's an exercise to make you more aware of their power. Tell a story you were told as a child, a fairy tale or a story from the Bible. Retell it with as much detail as you can.

Pick the big moment in the story and cavewrite about it. Here's my cavewrite about the Old Testament story, the binding of Isaac (page 133). As a child this story always horrified me and my cavewrite expresses my childhood concerns about the cruelty of God's command to Abraham. Let your cavewrite reflect your childhood feelings about the story.

Digging Deeper

Why did you choose that particular story? In what ways do you see the story differently now.

Resolving Old Stories

That God would ask Abraham to sacrifice his only son seemed a horrible thing. I remember when my mother told me the story. She read it from a Bible for young people that had these gaudy color illustrations. Isaac was strapped to the rock and Abraham was about to slit his throat with a dagger.

There was little I could do to see the sparing of Isaac as an act of mercy. But years later when I was studying anthropology, I read about how common human sacrifice was at the time. In this light, God's sparing Isaac was a message from a new God who was setting a new standard of behavior. Now it seems to me to be a story as

much about God's love as Abraham's obedience.

Stories change in the telling. They grow simpler and more powerful and no interpretation is entirely right. But we learn about ourselves when we study our interpretations of stories. Recently I wrote the following poem about Daniel and the lion's den. I thought of what it would be like to be Daniel in an open pit under the starry heavens.

In the Lion's Den
    A roaring sun
    a purring moon
    a future carved

on the surface of a wet tongue

There is no road to faith
only this cage
with the open ceiling

A twitching star
a twinkling tooth

Eyes that crave
raw meat and mercy.

When I read the newspaper, I realized Daniel's plight was a lot
like mine. As humans we are alone in a bestial jungle, but our faith
can transform that world. Daniel could see into the souls of the
beasts and they responded with gentleness instead of natural cruelty. My poem connects my life with a story thousands of years old.
Try a trigger or two to get you recycling the old stories.

Triggers

• Locate the core moment in an old story. Explode it on the
page or cavewrite it.
  • Tell an old story from a different point of view.
  • Tell an old story to your children.
  • Retell an old story as a short poem. Make every word count.
(You may want to focus on the core moment of the story.)
  • Draw a picture of an old story. Enter the story imaginatively,
focusing on the thing that has always intrigued you the most.
  • Find a child and a folktale. Tell the child the same story ten
times. Each time, revise the story in some way.
  • Draw a picture of two conflicting emotions. Write a poem
about your picture.
  • Write a fairy tale with three endings. Let your children decide
which one they like best.
  • Draw a tree that changes into a person, a person that changes
into an animal, or an animal that changes into a cloud. Give yourself
permission to enjoy that moment in your drawing where the change
occurs.
  • Invite a group of friends to your house for a special story circle.

Tell some old stories and talk about what they mean to you.

Dream Cycles

Primitive peoples viewed their dreams as messages from the spirit world. Like story cycles, these messages, revealed over and over in different ways, help dreamers to understand and come to terms with their lives. Interpreting the emotional message in our dreams is the first step in this process of self-discovery.

I have had several dreams about my father since he died. Each dream seems to pull at something deep inside me. I've recounted them here with an explanation of what I think they mean to me. I recounted the first dream in Chapter 3, but I've repeated it here so you can see it in the context of the others.

I am on the landing of the house on Highland Street, the first house I ever lived in. My father is a young man again and I am so happy to see him. He is wearing a tank-top undershirt and he has just shaved. I am hugging him and I can feel tears in my eyes. "Daddy! Daddy!" I shout. Suddenly I remember he is dead. I share this information with him. "You're dead, aren't you?" He nods his head sadly, looking down at the wooden floor. I wake up.

This dream was reassuring. My father appears as a young man, the young father who I depended on as a boy, not the old man who I became independent from. I'm so happy to see him, and even though I realize he is dead, his appearance in the dream contradicts that fact. I woke up realizing that my father is still a very large part of me even though he is gone.

In my second dream my father was staying at a four-star hotel in Honolulu. He met me in the lobby and told me about how wonderful his room was. He was anxious to share it with me, like a young child wanting to share a special treat. As he started to walk up a winding staircase I realized I couldn't follow him.

This dream reassured me that my father was OK. He was the older father who I loved from a distance. Death was not such a terrible thing; in fact, it was wonderful, only he couldn't share it with me. I would have to wait.

The next dream was about my sense of injustice at his dying. I am going to pick up the old Chevy Caprice, the car whose rusted-out body I had restored years ago. But the woman at the front desk says that I am too late, that they own the car now because I didn't come to pick it up. I am furious and I don't know what to do. I go out to see my father and he tells me he will settle this. He takes the piece of paper from my hands and goes into the building to argue. In my last image I see him inside at the desk with the paper in his hands.

My dreams tell me the many things that I feel about my father's death. They also point the way to a deeper understanding of who I am. When I listen to my dreams, my grief has a voice. A little research and I can connect that voice with what Elizabeth Kubler Ross calls the stages of grief.

Denial: Oh you're dead, aren't you?

Anger: Why did you leave me?

Bargaining: That lady can't steal the car. It's not fair.

Acceptance: You're dead, aren't you? The way my father looks down at the floor.

In the next section of this chapter we explore the connection between recurring dreams and recycled stories.

Crossing the Bridge

In my dream I was asked to drive over the General Sullivan Bridge without a car. I was not allowed to go on the road but required to crawl over the arched steel girders. It was a windy day and two hundred feet beneath me was the seventh strongest current in the world. The General Sullivan Bridge spans the distance between Newington and Dover, New Hampshire, the town where I was born.

I have had these dreams since I was a boy, but each one is different. Sometimes I am walking on tightropes, sometimes I am trying to balance on wooden beams, sometimes I am crawling on rubbery vines. I am always going somewhere important. I am always sure I will not make it but I will die trying. I always wake up frozen in terror at the moment when I cannot possibly proceed any further.

Stop right now and make a list of scary dreams you have had in your life. Pick one and make a quick cavewrite of the scariest moment in the dream. Now stop and freewrite about what you think the dream tells you about yourself.

Next write about a frightening moment in your life. Freewrite for ten minutes, then write about what you think that moment means.

Digging Deeper

Was it easy to remember your dreams? Have you had similar dreams since? How have your dreams changed over the years? Share your dreams with family or friends. Can they identify with your dreams?

The Bigger Picture

Writing down childhood fears helps us to understand them. I made a list of every fear I could remember: the Hollywood Indians from my childhood who impaled me with arrows, the Chinese communists from the cover of *Life* magazine who shot my father, the red devil from the turpentine can who threatened to eat me.

I decided to do some firewriting about what it was like to have a bad dream as a child.

There was a wooden hallway with a night-light outside my bedroom. I remember walking, feet on the hard floor, then opening the door to my parents' room and waiting for one of them to stir. I crawled in beside my mother, not moving, the animal warmth from her body like a soothing tonic. Bad dreams are always about being alone, and loneliness is something we are taught as children.

This last sentence jumped out at me. It seemed true, yet it surprised me when I wrote it. Maybe I didn't really need to write about fear, but about this loneliness. I started asking questions. Is this loneliness cultural? Do children in other countries experience this same loneliness?

Fear is an emotion that everyone feels but usually hides. It's passed down silently from generation to generation and only through the telling and retelling of our fearful stories do we break down the isolation and break the chain.

When Deborah Gulliver wrote a first draft of her book *The Night Rape* (Bristol, Vt., Opening Doors Books), the fear was still buried. Her book begins:

> My nightmare began one August night in 1986. I was working in a cafeteria-style restaurant. I worked as a dishwasher. We worked all night until about 2 A.M. I was

the only woman working in the dishroom that night.

I took the trash down and left it where it went. I started to go upstairs. I was standing in front of the elevator when a man grabbed me from behind.

There were two men because they were talking to each other. The man held a knife to my throat. His voice was so deep that when he spoke it went right through my head like a crack of thunder.

"If you scream we will kill you."

Her book tells about her rape and the long struggle to recover. She had gone to counseling but never really began to get over her fear until she wrote her story for everyone to hear. Apart from the therapeutic value, Deborah wrote her story so that other women who have had similar experiences won't blame themselves. I was in the room when Deborah read her first draft to her writing group. One of the women burst out into tears when Deborah read a section near the end of her story.

But please, my fellow victims, don't try to deal with it on your own because it will eat away at your brains and maybe, you will get to the point of believing it's your fault and you feel so ashamed that you try foolish things like taking your own life. Believe me it's much better to talk about it than keep it locked up in your mind. Use that key and let it out.

After she finished reading, Deborah met with the woman who had left the room. They talked and somehow they were not so alone anymore.

Writing is more than private therapy. It can connect us with those who share similar problems. It is a way of giving back and educating. When we write down the stories we have told and retold many times we begin to give a shape to our process of healing. And when people read our stories we give them a chance to share in the same process.

My dreams about the bridge stopped one night a few years ago. I was in the middle of the bridge alone. It was windy and I kept looking at the gray waves far underneath. I was terrified and I crouched to my knees. Then I realized there were people behind me. I was leading them across. If I didn't move they would all die.

I took one step, then another and another. The train of people followed me. Finally, after I'd walked several steps, I wasn't afraid anymore. I crossed the General Sullivan Bridge and I helped other people to cross, too.

I'm not sure if this dream is about learning to overcome isolation, but I know that once I thought of the people behind me, my own paralyzing fear seemed less important. I think about the bridge whenever it seems impossible to share feelings, whenever I want to just run away and live alone in some cabin in the woods, or simply in my own head. I think about the people behind me in the dream and it helps me to remember I am not alone; we are all trying to cross the bridge together.

Triggers

* Draw a picture of a place from one of your dreams.
* Trace your hand onto a piece of paper. Write a word for each finger and a word for your palm. Now make a fist and read the poem you wrote three times. Say the words a little louder each time.
* Write about a time someone hurt you.
* Write a letter to someone who hurt you and that you have never forgiven. Explain exactly how you were hurt and then forgive the person. Wait a day or two, then read the letter. Feel what it would be like to mail it and write about that. Decide whether or not to send it.

Find the moment in your story that you tend to lie about. Explode that one moment, reflecting about why you lied about it.

* Tell an imaginary story about a character who does the right thing. Rewrite it so they do the wrong thing.
* Pretend you are a character in an old story. Retell it from another point of view.

Writing Roots: Recycling History

In this chapter we've explored the introspective power of our unconscious minds to work through problems over and over, to seek resolution and make connections with the larger world. We have probed the mysteries of our past, our family and our dreams, and in our explorations we have perhaps uncovered new mysteries and new questions. I've illustrated the evolving nature of stories and given you tools to trace a story's path through time.

This final exercise is aimed at probing deeper into our family history.

1. Research your roots a generation or two back on both sides of your family. Interview your parents or other relatives to get a clearer understanding of who they were and where they came from. After you have researched several people, make a list of their traits. List the questions you have about them. Now close your eyes for a minute or two and imagine one of the relatives that intrigued you the most.

2. Open your eyes and freewrite a snapshot of that person at some moment in his or her life. Give yourself permission to add more detail to your snapshot and make it come alive. Return there in your mind and recreate that place. For example:

> She stood on the deck of the steamship in her black
> dress. The ocean churned beneath the bow and some of
> the spray washed across her dark face. She wore a black
> dress and held a grey woolen blanket over her shoulder.

3. Now write about a problem your relative had. Climb inside that person's mind and write a thoughtshot of what he or she is thinking. For example:

> She was trying not to think of the village in Poland —
> of her mother in the kitchen kneading dough for the
> Sabbath loaves — of her father in the garden digging up
> carrots for the soup, his hands black with earth. She felt
> herself slipping into sadness.

4. Read what you wrote and think about your relative's life. Write a question about your relative that lingers in your mind. For example: How did she survive the isolation of coming to a new country all by herself?

5. Compare this question to questions that you've generated throughout this chapter about your own life. Freewrite for ten minutes.

6. (Optional) Write a letter to your relative about your life. Write a reply to the letter pretending you are that person.

Digging Deeper

Did you learn anything new from your interview? Was it easy to find out what interested you? Or, did it all seem the same? Does your snapshot make you want to write more about your character? Can you see a thread that connects you with the person you wrote about?

Where Is Your God, if We Can Do This?

Family histories are like mystery stories with hidden plot twists. The more we connect with our ancestors, the more we understand the unspoken legacies they passed down to us. I learned this in my late twenties when I began writing stories about the Holocaust.

"They hit your uncle with the end of a rifle butt and while he lay there bleeding to death they turned to your aunt and said, 'Where is your God if we could do this?' " My mother's voice tells the story and I am always a young boy listening, an imaginary refugee from Nazi Germany in a small New Hampshire town. I see the photos of the relatives—the dark eyes, the worried faces. "This was taken before the war," she says. "You see all these people are gone." She refers to a man with a dark beard, a woman with heavy eyebrows, a little boy in a sailor suit not smiling. She kept the photos in a carton up in the attic. I must have been five or six when I first discovered the dusty box that contained the photos of my murdered relatives. I'm thirty-six now and I'm still trying to comprehend the Holocaust.

I remember first trying to comprehend 6 million Jews. If you figure the average arm spread of one person to be 3 feet (a conservative estimate that compensates for young children) and multiply that 6 million times, you get 18 million feet. Divide that by 5,280 (the number of feet in a mile) and you come up with approximately 3,400 miles. I imagined Jews holding hands from New Foundland to Florida and back along Interstate 95. Old men, old women, children and parents, standing in the breakdown lane with piles of luggage beside them. It's a sunny day in my image and they are simply waiting silently in black suits as the cars and trucks blast by them.

OK, that was 6 million Jews, but what did that have to do with me, a young Jew growing up in New Hampshire? I didn't know. All I knew was that I needed to write about it because of the sound of my mother's voice and the helpless feeling it created in the pit of my stomach.

The first story I wrote was about meeting a Holocaust survivor at Disneyland. The main character was a young divorced Jewish man who wants to escape life for a day. When he meets Eva Schwartz, however, he is haunted by images of concentration camp gas chambers within the benign images of Disneyland. As a child he was haunted by the stories his mother told about her family's death in the gas chambers. He dreams he is in the gas chamber at Auschwitz with his grandmother but the gas is not poisonous. It smells like cotton candy. He tries to tell his aunts and uncles but they pay no attention. They go on dying right in front of him.

Another early story was about a young Jewish boy who was learning how to swim. Each time he went into the water he felt an unexplainable fear grip him. He was the first in his family to brave the fear and as an older man he realizes this fear has something to do with his parents' history. This story was partially autobiographical. I am the only one in my family who learned how to swim and I have always had the feeling that this fear was passed down from previous generations.

I wrote other stories about the Holocaust and each one dealt with the theme of fear and paralysis and how it filtered down into my generation. Each new story seemed to illuminate the historical terror just a tiny bit more.

What themes did you see in your family stories? How do they play out in your life today?

Triggers

• Interview your parents or grandparents. Find out as much as possible about their lives growing up. Research facts about the time when they grew up. Ask probing questions and gather some hard facts. Imagine you are a historical novelist gathering facts to make your characters believable. Next, take the point of view of one of your parents and recreate a scene from that parent's life in writing.

• Plot a four-generation best-selling novel about your family. The three main characters are three men or women in direct descendence from each other. The fourth is you or your parent.

Don't feel bound to the truth. Create new events or change real ones. You can stretch the truth to make the stories more dramatic.

For example: Great-grandmother is a prostitute in Victorian England, Grandmother is a nurse, Mother is a movie star and you are a musician.

Begin with a list of characters. Write a page or so about each one.

Describe them physically. Talk about their problems, their dreams, their fears, etc.

Then write an outline of the story, starting at the beginning and moving to the end. A plot outline is simply what happens in the story. For example:

> Sam is a worker in a nineteenth-century shoe factory.
> He meets Greta one day when she yells at him for work-
> ing too slowly. He doesn't like her, but he falls in love
> with her. They get married and live near the factory. . . .

As you plot your novel ask yourself some questions. What traits do these four people share? On what parts of their dreams have they compromised? What have they not compromised on? What physical genetic traits bind these four people?

- Create a psychological coat of arms for your family using the dominant emotions and images of your family as material.

- Dig through all your old photo albums and find a picture of a relative you never knew but who intrigues you. Place the photograph in front of you on the table. Freewrite about that person, including some description of the photograph. Write your relative a letter about your life.

- Make a story wheel with three family stories told by the same member of the family. Freewrite about some of the questions that emerge.

- Design a postcard that depicts a moment in your past. Pretend you have the power to time travel to that moment. Write a few quick perceptions of that moment on the postcard and send it back to yourself.

Then and Now

In this chapter we've learned to see how core stories grow when we tell and retell them. In the next chapter we reenter those stories with new eyes and add a new voice. But before we do, take a minute to look over the writing in your journal. Read a few stories that still intrigue you. Stop and ask yourself: "What do I know now that I didn't know then?"

Freewrite your answer at the top of a new blank page. In the next chapter we learn ways to reenter our stories with new eyes.

▪ Chapter 7 ▪

The Man Behind the Curtain: Intervening in the Past and Present

Vitally, the human race is dying. It is like a great uprooted tree, with its roots in the air. We must plant ourselves again in the universe.

—D.H. Lawrence

As we learn to play with points of view, we gain a flexibility of understanding that gives us a power we never had before when examining our past. In this chapter we explore techniques for reentering our stories and intervening with a newer, more mature perspective.

Finding the Real Wizard

Face a fear and the death of that fear is certain.

—Evie Malcolm

"Pay no attention to that man behind the curtain," says the Wizard of Oz in his thundering voice. The curtain blows around the frantic old man pulling the levers. Suddenly the terrifying Wizard is nothing more than a silly frightened man running a large machine and speaking into a microphone. "I am the great and powerful (the machine bellows) Wizard of Oz," the man says in his shaky apologetic voice.

It is my all-time favorite movie moment because it is so essentially human. We all have tyrannical voices like the wizard's in our brains. They don't think twice about calling us names, intimidating us into feeling inadequate, shaming us into submission. And yet how many of us have the opportunity to see the man or woman behind the curtain pulling the levers. In the last chapter we experimented with

144

seeing life from different points of view. Now let's begin locating the points of view in our own mind and learning how to intervene on them to make the future different than the past.

Who Tells Us Who We Are?

As we explore further, sooner or later we come in contact with the forces that shaped our own unique point of view. Understanding these forces is the beginning of true self-knowledge.

Here's an exercise to begin the process of identifying who told us who we are and learning to talk back to those voices.

The Definitive Chorus

1. Starting with your own family, make a list of all the people in your life who at one time or another told you who you are.

2. For each person write two or three sentences of them talking to you and telling you who you are. The lines can be positive or negative. Don't labor over this. Think of how each person defines you and write the first thing that comes into your head.

3. One by one, answer the definitive chorus. Try to keep your responses to a few sentences, but go deeper if the spirit moves you. For example:

> Mom: You never finish the milk with your cereal.
> (Get a life, Mom.)
> Dad: You're too sensitive.
> (Men have feelings too, Dad.)

Digging Deeper

Which people seem to define you the most? Which answers were the most fun to write? Try expanding one of your answers into a dialogue.

Talking Back to the Voices

If this exercise worked, you may have identified a voice in your head that, up until now, you thought was part of you. You thought you were a slob, but in reality it was just Aunt Margaret's voice telling you that you are a slob. "I'm not a slob, Aunt Margaret," you told her back. And from now on, whenever you notice the banana peel on the back seat floor of your car and the cloud of fruit flies that swarm around your hand as you pick it up, your mind will interrupt Aunt Margaret's voice instead of being crushed by it. "Yes, there is a banana peel on the back seat floor of my car. Yes, there are fruit flies swarming around it. But, *No! I am not a slob!!!! Understand, Aunt Margaret?*"

Learning to identify voices in our mind frees us to see beyond them. It liberates our minds from oppression.

Triggers

- Write a short play called *The Voices in My Head*.
- Draw masks for different emotions inside you. Draw one mask for you.
- Write about a time you surprised yourself and did something you didn't feel capable of doing.
- Write several snapshots of yourself from different times in your life. Give a voice to each snapshot.
- Do a sketch of your body on a big blank piece of paper. Like a cartoonist give a voice to different parts of your body. Make jokes, reminisce, cry, whine, sigh; do anything that comes to mind. Give voices to as many parts of your body as you can. Have them talk to each other.

Writing Down Voices

Givan Thompson is a motivational speaker who lectures on drug abuse and the power of positive thinking to high school students around the country. Halfway through a speech, he paused and asked students to whisper a name someone in their family had called them at some time in their life. As he wandered up and down the aisles of the auditorium, he listened and looked at the faces. When he got back up to the podium, he said, "You know it was sad for me to hear the terrible names you were called by people you love, and you know the saddest thing of all for me was looking at your faces when you said the name. I could tell that many of you still believed you were the name."

Writing down the voices can be a first step in seeing inside our own minds and learning to get distance.

1. Write down five names someone from your family called you that hurt your feelings. A name can be more than one word. It can

be a phrase that defines you. If you grew up in a perfect family, use names friends called you.

2. Find a corner and read your list out loud ten times, growing slightly louder each time. (Try doing this in your car if you are embarrassed.) In a group situation try reciting your names one person after the other. Shout them at each other. Feel the power of the words evaporate off your lips. Notice how repetition and listening to the words weakens even the cruelest insult, and sometimes even makes it funny.

3. Now take another minute and write down two or three personal weaknesses you have. Recite them ten times, getting louder each time. Now alternate between the insult and the weakness. For example: I'm disorganized.

> Slob
> I can't do math.
> Dumb shit

4. Listen to the voices. Give yourself time to feel the distance creep into your voice.

5. Draw a picture of the two voices. Show their relationship.

6. Now look at what you've written. Add a third voice, a voice of affirmation. Here's one: "I'm more than that."

Your affirmation must be totally positive. It mustn't argue; it should just state its undeniable claim: "You're better than that!" Repeat your affirmation three times. Say it with total commitment. Take a deep breath before each affirmation.

Now try all three. Find your own order. Try experimenting with where to interject affirmations. Like this:

> "You are so disorganized."
> "Slob!"
> "You're *more* than that!"

7. (Group option) With a group of people, try creating a chorus of affirmation and individuals to hurl insults and divulge weaknesses. With practice you can make it so the affirmations slowly drown out the other voices.

Digging Deeper

What did it feel like to write down your voices? What does it feel like to read the voices?

Rewriting the Opera in Our Minds

When I do this exercise with high school students I sometimes observe their process. They sit with the scrap of white paper in front of them. I can see the moment the hurtful word comes into their consciousness, then the next moment when they decide whether or not it is safe enough to write it down, then the final moment when they write it down and quickly fold it up.

I quickly gather up the scraps of paper in one hand. Then I stand in front of them and let the papers fall like snowflakes. "This is not you," I say. But when I look at their faces, like Givan Thompson, I can tell they don't believe me.

But later, when I manage to get a few brave souls to do the previous exercise in front of the class, I can see that a few of them are beginning to believe in the affirmation. The more we share our weaknesses and our pain, the less we are burdened by them.

I teach children to hear the opera that goes on in a human being's mind. We have voices hurling insults, whispering inadequacies, telling us in subtle ways that we're not good enough. Then we have the ability to rise above it all and see the truth.

One way to understand these voices is to write them down. When we acknowledge them we can begin to acknowledge that these voices are not us. We began this process in Chapter 5 when we split our personality, but now we are learning to imagine new voices that can intervene on the ones already there.

Triggers

- Collect a group of friends and act out each other's opera.
- Using a video camera and a group of friends, write a video poem where you cut between close-ups of people telling personal weaknesses, people being insulted and people affirming each other. Watch the video on the TV and notice how the faces take on the personality of the words. Know that words can heal.
- Put music to the voices and make a real opera. Don't worry if you sing off key. It's the expression that's important here. If you're alone, perform your opera into a tape recorder and play it back to yourself. In a group, assign different parts and sing the opera. Take time to direct your songs to get the full emotional effect. Have your friends take turns acting out their operas.

- Make a flag or design, a sort of personal coat of arms, that represents the voices in your head.
- Make a list of affirmations like, "You're more than that." Practice saying them at times of crisis.

Time-Traveling Detectives

You learn from the imaginative what the real world is.
—Bernard Malamud

It sometimes takes writers years to begin uncovering and writing about their deepest core stories. When Richard Rhodes won the Pulitzer prize in 1989 for his book, *The Making of the Atomic Bomb* (Touchstone Books), he had written eight books and had a successful career as a writer. He had also lost several marriages and had become a heavy drinker. At fifty-three he went into therapy. A short time after that he began to write *A Hole in the World* (Touchstone Books, 1990), an autobiographical memoir of his nightmarish childhood. In a recent interview he said, "For the first time in my life I'd begun writing about the events which underpin all my writing. . . . My writing was, in a way, an escape from these dark forces, and now I was confronting them head on."

In one section of *A Hole in the World*, Rhodes describes watching his abusive stepmother prepare to hit his older brother with the end of a mop handle. He remembers thinking how the blow would crack his brother's spine and leave him paralyzed. Forty years later, while doing research for his memoir, he interviewed his brother and discovered he was actually the one hit with the mop handle. He had rewritten the scene in his memory to distance himself from the pain. Only when he tried to reenact the scene did he uncover the real truth.

In a way, all autobiographical writers are time-traveling detectives. We go back in time gathering leads, clues and more information from different sources. We take everything we have learned since and reenter our lives. So far in this chapter we've been practicing ways to reenter our lives and intervene. In this section we are going to have some fun with this concept.

Look through your journal at exercises from the early part of the book. Pick an incident from your writing or simply think of one.

Try to make it a painful or puzzling incident. List a few before you pick one. Now close your eyes and imagine you are a private eye. You drink heavily. You've spent a lifetime running away from your problems. You've been through several marriages or you have avoided marriage altogether.

It is the year 2010 and you have finally sought therapy. Your therapist has pinpointed the problem and booked you on a time-travel flight to your youth. You are told just to observe things and ask questions to the suspects involved, including yourself. Write a short account of your trip. Give yourself time to play around with characters and situations. You may want to begin by simply describing yourself to the reader.

If you feel it's too difficult to create a whole piece, try simply to write a dialogue between your younger self and your older self about a specific incident or time.

Digging Deeper

How would you define the relationship between your older self and your younger self? Which self do you identify with more? Why? Does this encounter tell you anything about the process of aging?

The Case of the Lost Naiveté

Here's my piece where I go back to college days to the night my first girlfriend betrayed me and slept with my ex-roommate.

It takes me back to the summer of 1976. I remember the night well. I had called her house all evening. She had gone to Greg's for dinner. Greg had just broken up with his girlfriend. I kept calling and her roommate would answer. "She's not home yet," the roommate would say. I rode my bicycle five miles in the dark, without a light, to her house. I lay there for hours waiting.

> I was trying to find something I lost. Was it lost or was it stolen? It was my naiveté. At least I thought it was mine. A young man was laying on a bed. He had long hair. He looked like me and he looked like someone just snapped the head off his pet turtle.
> "What the hell are you doing here?" I say to him.
> "I'm waiting for her."
> "You're killing yourself. Go home."

"Maybe."

"You know where she is."

"I do. She's at Greg's. She went there for dinner."

"She doesn't love you."

"I don't believe that."

He rolls over. I go downstairs and make myself a cup of tea. It's an old house with uneven wooden floors and a smell of camphor. I made love for the first time on that bed upstairs. I will meet the guy she is making love to three years from now in a supermarket. He is my ex-roommate from my freshman year of college. He is from New Jersey and taught me transcendental meditation. I'll make conversation with him and all the time I will have a funny, sad feeling.

If I could get the grieving young man to leave now instead of waiting till Greg drops her off in the morning, I could save the kid some pain. But the kid seems to like pain. That's the funny thing. He doesn't know how to protect himself.

Here he comes now for another cup of tea. He won't sleep tonight. He'll go for walks into town. He'll look up at the half-moon. He'll make wishes on stars that don't fall.

"Who the hell are you," he says. "Where did you come from?"

"What's more important is where I've been," I say. "I know your problems. You need to learn how to protect yourself."

"You don't seem like a very happy person to me."

"I'm as happy as you'll ever get."

"Want a cup of tea?"

"As long as it's not red zinger."

"That's all we have. How did you know that?"

"I know a lot of things."

I look at him. He's wearing those old ratty jeans I used to wear. He's looking at me and I can see a strange confusion in his eyes. It's like he knows who I am but he won't let himself understand.

"Let me tell you something. Four years from now

you'll take her to a movie. She will have been married
and divorced. She'll tell you that you seem older, but that
out of all the men she'd ever been with you were the only
one she ever thought about seeing again. You'll look at
her and wonder what you ever saw there. You'll realize
all this stuff right now is about you—not him, not her.
You!"

"What the hell are you, the ghost of Christmas future?"

"Very funny. Keep laughing."

"I mean it, why did you come here tonight? Are you
my fairy godfather?"

"Sure, if you want me to be."

"I want you to leave."

I looked at him. I know what pain is. I've learned to
hide from it well. This guy takes it all on the chin. He
lets the bull gore him over and over. I was him. It's hard
to believe it. I was him.

My little sketch reminds me of how little I protected myself back
then. My private eye is fascinated by that. I suspect it reminds him
a little of a trusting self he has lost. My younger self doesn't understand his cynicism, yet he is encountering the forces that helped to
mould it. What did your private eye find?

We return to find out what really happened. This can be, in turns,
both frightening and enlightening. But the more we write, the more
our fears and insights are known to us, and there is a possibility for
healing and self-discovery.

Triggers

• Send your time-traveling detective back into one of your core
stories. Have the detective report about the real situation.

• Write an action scene where your detective encounters one of
your arch enemies from the past.

• Write a dialogue between your older self and your younger
self. Have them discuss an unresolved issue.

• Think of a place from your past that has a lot of meaning
and memory. Send your detective back there and have him or her

describe it physically. Try not to have the detective describe his or her feelings about the place, rather let these leak through in the description.

- Send your detective into your school, have him or her confront a teacher you had problems with. Have the detective rescue your younger self from some peril.

Reparenting the Inner Kid

If your detective had trouble figuring out what to investigate, this exercise might help. It's a variation of work done by John Bradshaw in his book *Homecoming* (Bantam, 1990).

1. Write the word *unresolved* on a blank piece of paper and web all the things in your life that today remain unresolved.

2. Pick one event from your web and freewrite for ten minutes.

3. Stop. Write the following question on the top of a blank page in your journal: What do I know now that I didn't know then?

4. Freewrite for ten minutes answering this question.

5. Write a dialogue between you now and you then.

Digging Deeper

Was it easy to answer the question in step 3 or did you have to stop and think? Why did you pick the issue that you did? What will you learn in another ten years about this event?

Interrupting the Past

Bob is a twenty-four-year-old student in one of my prison writing classes who had never spoken or written much about his parents' death until he wrote the following piece:

My Life

The day was October 28, 1973 and I got out of bed to help set up an anniversary party for my parents. It was their eleventh anniversary and my sister, brother and myself had, with the help of my grandparents, rented a hall for the party.

My parents loved the party very much but they had to leave a little early because they had made reservations at a restaurant the previous day.

They went to dinner in Burlington and they had drunk a lot. Dad wasn't feeling that great and wasn't well enough to drive home. They still got into the car and tried to drive home anyway, instead of calling someone to pick them up. It was a little after 11 P.M. when they had called home and said they should be home shortly.

A little after 11:30 P.M. there was a knock on the door. I got up from watching a rerun of "Spiderman" on TV to answer the door. I opened the door to see a man in a uniform standing there. I was only five at the time so I didn't know what to do. So I yelled to my grandmother who was over babysitting. I heard them talking low about my parents. I can't recall all the words the man said but some of the words I can remember were words like "accident," "car wrecked," "people dead." Right then I knew something was wrong with my parents.

They were going around some very sharp curves in a place they call Granville Gulf. They had been speeding to see if they could make it home sooner. My Dad had lost control of the car and it went over a bank. Ma was thrown out of the car through the windshield because she wasn't wearing her seat belt. Dad had been crushed between the seat and the steering wheel when the car hit a tree. They were both killed instantly so at least they didn't die with a lot of pain.

Three days after my parents died we had the funeral. That was a real sad day for the family. I was very sad to see my parents in those coffins being lowered into that black hole. I cried for the next two days.

The day after the funeral I was sent into an adoption home. I really didn't know what was to come of that. I was placed in three foster homes over the next two years. I acted like a little hellion who didn't want to stay with anyone who was not my parents.

Finally a family came to the home who was looking for a seven-year-old to adopt. I fell in love with this family and knew I wanted to be adopted by them. The only conflict was that I had a twin brother and they only wanted one child. So, after going through hell, I was finally adopted by them. I haven't seen my twin brother in over ten years now and I'm not even sure he is alive.

I got to this place in Hancock, Vermont, and the house looked very nice but I still missed my parents' home. I really didn't know what was to come of all this. I was very happy, but very sad at the same time. When I finally got enough nerve to speak I told my stepparents that it would be a while before I could call them Mom and Dad. They said that they understood.

It took me five months before I would call my stepparents Mom and Dad. And when I finally did say it I was very glad I had a Mom and Dad I could love again.

Bob ended his first draft of the story here with this somewhat happy ending. Through conversation I found out that Bob is in jail for stealing property from his stepfather. I asked him to reflect a little about what he knows now about his story that he didn't know back then. This is what he wrote.

Having parents die when you're at a young age is not easy for you, but as you grow older you try and figure out stuff about your parents and that makes it very hard to get over the loss of your parents.

I have a hundred different pictures of my parents hanging on my walls. A few of them are taken with the whole family together and my parents' wedding day. There are also newspaper clippings of my parents' accident hanging on the wall. Somedays I sit at the kitchen table and wonder what it would be like to see them again and what they would be like. I know I will be reunited with them someday and we will be once again one big happy family. A Dad, a Mom and their kids.

To this day I believe they are in heaven looking over me and trying to help me turn my life around. It makes me very happy to know they still love me.

I have lived the past seventeen years with a sad memory of my parents. I hope I never will forget them. I don't think I ever will.

The more Bob writes his story, the more he begins to unravel its effect on his life. He feels an intense loyalty to his natural parents and at the same time is afraid of forgetting them. If Bob had a normal upbringing he would be at an age where he would be breaking away from his parents. But, how can he ever grow up when his parents are the same — in his mind — as they were when he was five?

Bob writes about wanting to know what they would be like today. He needs to see his parents' evolving view of him so he can grow up. They have to be up there watching him or he will forever be that five-year-old boy waiting for them to come home. Bob's writing has given him a way of expressing and rethinking a wound he has carried around most of his life. The words not only connect him with what happened, but help him to discover how he has survived and how he can continue to survive.

Finding the truth can often be painful, but is it any more painful than living a lie for years?

Jon is a basic writer in one of my classes. Because of learning disabilities he will never get his high school equivalency degree, but this doesn't stop him from writing many pages. Recently he wrote a long piece detailing all his childhood injuries in graphic detail. Here is an example of two incidents:

> A good friend of mine and I was sitting on my aunt's front porch when his brother came along throwing a stick up in the air and letting it hit the ground. I heard him calling my name. As I turned to look at him, he threw the stick at a fork that had its fingers up in the air. It got me in the right eye and tear duct, which was pushed deep into the cheek of my face. As the doctor in the hospital went to pull out the fork, the blood began to run down my face and into my mouth.
>
> Then in 1965 came my next battle scar. It was from a knife a friend and I were using to play chicken with. I put the knife right through my thumb, and it was sticking two inches out the other side. The blood was pouring off my hand.

Eight similar incidents followed. When he was done, his writing group asked that he write a few paragraphs on why he thought all these injuries kept happening to him. At first he kept saying, "I like to bleed. If I had a knife right now I'd probably cut myself." All the time he laughed about this paper, and kept asking, "Do you want more gore?" "No," we said. "We want the truth." "You want the truth, do you?" he said.

It took him two hours to write these two paragraphs and when he was done he said, no longer laughing nervously, "I think I have something here."

> I thought that I would write about something that I had done over the last twenty years of my life and see if I could understand me and how I lived my life so you could see that I didn't turn out like other kids did. My mother gave me everything I wanted but she never gave me love. So when I got my first cut now I was a person and could bleed like everyone in the world.
>
> When I got the next one I knew that this was not going to be the last because that one was not planned out, but it happened. My Aunt Kath said you have to go home, so I did that one out of spite to them.
>
> If I was to go out of jail now I don't need any more cuts because I have too many now and I don't like them anymore.
>
> I don't like how I am so I tried to break him down so he can cry like a person.

Jon has begun to solve his mystery. He has learned something about the motive behind all these bloody accidents. It was partly for spite and partly to make up for the lack of love in his family. Ironically, you could say these accidents were Jon's way of healing an imbalance in his childhood. Interestingly enough, it is at the point Jon begins to become honest and self-reflective that he begins talking in the third person. "I don't like how I am so I try to break him down so he can cry like a person." Pain makes us all yearn for distance, but how can we begin to heal if we don't admit to the wound?

As writers we are capable of solving old crimes and interpreting past motives. Our lives are scattered with clues and evidence. When we write, we dust for fingerprints; we review mug shots; we grab our younger selves by the lapels, pin them against a wall and bark through clenched teeth, "Give it to me straight this time!"

And once we begin to unravel the mysteries of our youth, the newer, more complex mysteries of our current age make themselves known.

Triggers

• Just for a moment imagine you can go back in history and correct any of life's injustices. Think of one particular moment. Start with a list of details, then write for ten minutes about that moment in time.

• Draw a time line of all the important moments in your parents' lives. Important moments are those that contain decisions that set their life in a certain direction: marriage, divorce, travel, etc. Return to one of those moments.

• Think of a period in your life that you can characterize by a feeling: "the carefree days of the summer of '82," or "the sad winter of 1990." Brainstorm a list of details from that time and write a description of the time you choose.

• Pretend you have gone on a vacation to a past part of your life. Draw a postcard that depicts a scene from that period in your life. Write a note to yourself on the other side. Send it to yourself.

• Make a list of rules with the heading, "How to Survive Childhood."

• Write a letter with your opposite hand (left if you are right-handed or right if you are left-handed). Pretend your inner child is writing the letter. What does the child have to ask or tell you? Hold the letter for a day or two and think about it. Then respond with your dominant hand.

Intervening With the Imagination: The Great Healer

Another way to intervene in our past is with our imagination. This exercise teaches you to see the survival value of fantasy.

1. Think of a period of crisis in your life. Go back there in your mind.

2. Think of a problem you have right now. Fantasize an answer to the problem.

3. Look at what you wrote and ask yourself where your fantasy came from.

4. Add three details to your fantasy to make it come alive more.

Digging Deeper

How does your fantasy grow out of reality? Which details make it come alive the most? How does your fantasy make you feel?

The Power of Fantasy

Anja Kuperman was a sixteen-year-old Jewish girl living in hiding in Lublin, Poland. Her entire family was taken to a death camp one day when she was at work. She wrote her feelings in her diary. I've known Anja since I was a young boy growing up in Dover, New Hampshire, and ever since then she has been telling her story in whatever language, in whatever way, she can. As you read the following excerpt from Anja's journal, notice how her ability to fantasize feeds her spirit.

I woke up one early morning during springtime; looked out of the window and saw a very peaceful nature world — beautiful blue sky, birds were singing their songs, trees and flowers in bloom, sun shining which made the colors come out more to their beauty; a real joy to the eye . . .

The sunray comes through the window and warms the room; what a beautiful world. . . . But, for me personally there is no meaning or fulfillment in all that beauty; no joy, no hope, no future. The warm sunrays come through the window and warm up my room, however in my heart it is cold. I am living in fear of my life, the sunrays cannot warm up my inner being. I lost trust in people and humanity. The world is full of hate, uncaring, selfishness and indifference. I am all alone in the world; nobody to talk to, no one to trust, no one to love or care. I live from hour to hour, unsure of what the day or night will bring; the next hour could bring me death. Will there be another tomorrow?

Memories from my past come forward into my thoughts; my dear father and mother who loved me so much, family and friends, it was too much . . . tears and sorrow with pain in my heart breaks me down. . . . Oh people can you understand to live alone in emptiness and danger? Being only sixteen-years-old, seeing the surrounding beauty of nature and then not having the

right to enjoy God's creation; what have I done wrong?
I was born Jewish, is that wrong? Why? . . . Can that be
explained to me? Death is my sentence. . . . I have no
right to live. I am also one of God's creation. I like to see
the sun, the moon, stars, pick flowers and enjoy life. . . .
I'm part of this planet.

I miss so much my mother and father, friends and
family; someone to give me hug and kiss and tell me "I
love you." Not all that hate and degrading I have to endure; I like to be myself.

When it's dark I live in a big fantasy; no one is better
than me. I forced the Nazis out of Poland; put them in
concentration camps and let people live in peace. However, came day again, reality told me different. I was one
of the hounded people; I was the one who was suffering
from the Nazi plague. Oh how I wished to have the
power to do the same to the Nazis that they do to us;
throw bombs on their cities, let them suffer, tear their
families apart, then send them away to no return.

My heart cries for justice and peace; will it ever come?
Peace, love, joy . . . no pain, no hurt.

Sometimes I dream to be a princess; the people are
listening to me, I have confidence in myself and people
are loving each other and caring for each other.

Fantasy can remove us, even for a few moments, from a desperate
situation and give our heart solace. Look at your own power to
fantasize and remember it is a tool that can help you retrieve hope.

Triggers

• Close your eyes and imagine what it would feel like to be taken
care of. Make a list and add to it throughout the day. Find one thing
on your list that you can do for yourself. Do it.

• Imagine a world with no money problems. Freewrite about a
normal day.

• Retell a core story letting your imagination take over to rewrite
it into a happy ending.

• Cavewrite a fantasy of a perfect life. Put in as much detail as
you can.

• Think of a moment in your past when you failed yourself. Go back to that moment and rewrite the scene with you as the hero. Note that the power we have to reimagine the past is the same power that will transform the future.

Scenes From a Mirage: Reimagining the Present

Now that we've learned to use our imagination as a tool for understanding the past we are ready to apply this tool to the present.

1. Think of an emotionally charged scene that repeats itself over and over again in your household. If you are married, it may be a fight with your spouse or your children. If you are living at home it may be scenes with roommates or siblings. Find one scene and locate it in time and place. Where does it take place? What is the situation? How does it start? How does it end? Freewrite for ten minutes answering some of these questions.

2. Now begin the scene by writing at least three pages of dialogue, making sure you double-space each line.

3. Add snapshots to your scene to make it come alive. For example:

"Shut up," she said. She stood by the green refrigerator, a carton of milk in her hands.

4. Add thoughtshots of just your own thoughts. For example:

"I'm leaving," I said. I could feel a volcano erupting inside. You're not gonna let this happen, the voice kept repeating, you're not gonna let her say that to you.

5. Reread your scene. If possible read it through with the person you wrote it about, or act it out in front of your writing group with a group member playing the second role.

6. Freewrite about what you learned from this exercise.

7. (Optional) Rewrite this scene as a parody by exaggerating the dialogue and actions of your characters. (See creating satirical voices, Chap. 5.)

8. Based on what you've learned, rewrite your role in the scene in a way that will change the outcome positively. Make sure you fully imagine how your partner will react to your new lines and actions.

Digging Deeper

What did it feel like to write down the scene? Did you find yourself getting angry when you acted out the scene? Did you gain anything from writing down this scene? If so, what?

Did You Forget Your Lines or What?

Imagine this scenario. A husband is having a fight with his spouse. She has just thrown bagels at him and he is heading out the door. Suddenly he turns to his wife and says, "I'm sorry." "You can't be sorry enough," the wife says. The husband stops. "I had no right to hurt your feelings like that. I'm really sorry."

"You don't mean it. I can tell by your voice," she replies.

"Fine," he says and walks out the door, slamming it behind him.

Now let's rewrite the scene from the line before it ended. Let's revise the man's anger.

"You don't mean it. I can tell by your voice."

"I do mean it. I really do."

"You don't. If you were really sorry you'd apologize."

"I'm sorry I forgot our anniversary."

"I can't believe you forgot our anniversary. I just can't believe it. That really hurt my feelings."

"I'm sorry I hurt your feelings."

"You don't care about me."

"I do care about you. I really do."

Explosive scenes often end too early. They depend on predictable patterns of the actors. They depend on a general sense of our powerlessness and a retreat into defensive postures. Beneath our anger lies sadness and fear. Intervening on our anger is often the process of being emotionally honest with ourselves instead of blaming or competing with the other.

In her book, *The Dance of Anger,* Harriet Goldhor Lerner (New York: Harper & Row, 1986), shows how one member can change the whole direction of a scene by refusing to play an old role and by taking on a newer, more assertive role. Learner shows couples that though they can't control their partner's behavior, they can control their own. Learning to intervene on your thoughts and emotions is the first step in writing a new role for yourself. Practice the next time an all-too-predictable scene plays itself in your home.

Triggers

- Rewrite a scene from your partner's point of view.
- Rewrite a scene from work to create a more positive outcome. Define the key moment in the scene and remember it when you go to work.
- Write an explosive scene from your childhood about your parents. Add your own voice to the scene as an adult—not as a child. Tell your parents what you see and what they do not see. Tell them the effect they are having on your life. Tell them anything you want to tell them.
- Rewrite a scene from a troubling dream so that is has a less troubling outcome. Define the key moment in the scene where you intervened.

The Big Picture: Connecting With the Larger World

Insist on Joy in spite of everything.
—Tom Robbins

As we listen and intervene on the voices in our heads and learn to share our discoveries with others, something amazing happens— we begin to see that our own suffering is not so unique. There are patterns connecting us with others who have suffered similar injuries and there are professionals who have spent years studying them. Researching your pain can be an important way to connect with the larger world and to find a collective voice to add to the others you have defined. This exercise is aimed at helping you to realize the power of seeing the big picture.

1. Write *pain* in capital letters on a blank page in your journal.

2. Pick one emotional injury you would like to explore further. Go to the library and find a book that deals with the injury in some way. It can be a psychology book, a novel, a children's book, even a song. Find someone in the big world who shared a similar experience.

3. Freewrite for ten minutes comparing your life to the research you have found.

Digging Deeper

What did it feel like to find someone who had a similar experience? Or were you unable to find anyone? How does your experience differ from the experience of the person you found? How is it similar? What is the advantage of looking beyond our own lives?

Voices at the Library

Jane was in her fifties when she first realized she had grown up in an alcoholic family. Her realization came through writing several essays in freshman English class, two of which are quoted in Chapter 1 of this book. Jane decided to do her research paper on the children of alcoholics. The more research she did, the more she understood her father's and mother's abusive behavior within a new context. For the first time she learned that it was not unusual for children of alcoholics to think there was nothing wrong. Denial is the most common response of children who desperately want their parents to love them. "It never occured to me," Jane says in her paper. "I didn't connect violent mood swings and violent behavior with drinking. I truly did not think drinking alcohol was any different than say, drinking Pepsi."

Studying research on children of alcoholics helped Jane to see that the emotional neglect she suffered as a child had a cause that went beyond the assumption that her parents were cruel or there was something wrong with her. Though her pain was still there, she gained a framework of interpreting it that connected with thousands of others who shared the same experience. Instead of creating affirming voices, Jane found them at the library.

Triggers

• Think of a situation where you act in a way you'd like to change. Create the situation in writing with yourself being a third-person character. Give your character thoughts that will allow him to act in a new way.

• Write five questions about a subject you want to know more about. Pick the most intriguing and write for ten minutes trying to answer it. Next, go to the library and research the answer to your question. Write for another ten minutes comparing your answer with the research.

• Find a cookbook containing food you have never eaten. Wait until you are hungry and find a recipe. Follow the recipe and make the dish. Close your eyes when you taste it. Delight in your power to try new things.

• Write the first chapter of a historical novel set in a time you would like to study. Go to the library and research the period. Using your research try to make the period in history come alive with detail.

• Pick a subject to research. Find ten facts about your subject. Turn those facts into a poem.

• Make a list of all the unanswerable questions you can think of. Pick one and go to the library to find books that try to answer it. Write about what you find.

The Detour Less Traveled: Intervening With Cartoons

1. Pick the most serious painful thing in your life, something that has hurt you for years and limited your capacity to dream and imagine yourself differently. Write it down in as few words as possible on a piece of paper:

Shyness

Insecurity

An inability to organize

Sadness about unfulfilled expectations

2. Make several photocopies of the figure on the next page.

Take one and fill in the blank on the road sign. Make the figure in the car like yourself and make a road to the left for a detour. Know that you are behind the wheel. You have feet and hands and fingers gripping the wheel. You are in control.

Hang your cartoon near your writing desk or on the refrigerator. Think of the changes you are already making in your life.

The Foundations of New Worlds

My father's voice tells me many things. I hear it more now that he is gone. Sometimes I listen. Sometimes I talk back. I did a cavewrite of my father's voice. In that cavewrite I see my father telling

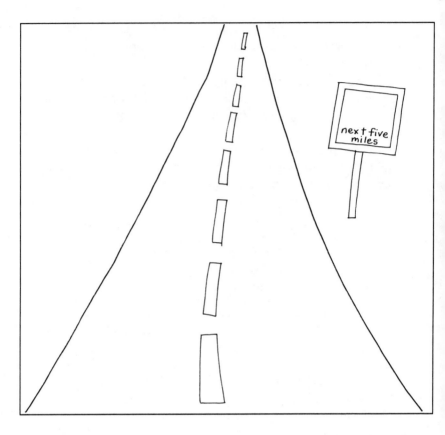

me to take it easy, that everything is OK, not to get aggravated, not to get overheated.

When I talk to that voice I not only feel close to my father, I feel closer to myself. But sometimes I don't hear that voice. I am trapped in my own head; my father's voice is indistinguishable from my own. That's when it's time to practice what we've learned in this chapter. That's when I need to interrupt the voice.

Lately I haven't been taking care of myself. I have many excuses, one of which is writing this book. I stay up late. I drink a lot of coffee. I overeat the wrong foods. The other day my wife, Carollee, said, "Your father died a year ago, the week you started working on the book. I was sick and we had a three-week-old baby. You had no time or space to grieve. Don't you think that maybe you are still trying to get over his death?"

I thought about what she said. I thought of how my father never took care of himself. Abusing my health was a way of feeling closer to him. I made a list of my needs and made a commitment to start fulfilling them.

Your writing can help you do the same. You can learn to intervene on your thoughts and feelings. You have the power to interrupt the past so it does not become the future. We have seen that intervening on the voices in our minds is the first step in creating new lives and new worlds to live in.

We explore these new lives in the final chapter of the book. But, before we get there, take a break. Look back through your journal and marvel at all the writing you have done. Give yourself permission to enjoy passages and linger over them. Know that your writing is precious, something no one can take away from you. Feel the power you have to intervene on your thoughts, memories and imaginations. You can revise the world, and you have already begun. New worlds are growing inside you. Are you ready to explore them?

Try this. Write *Joy* on a blank page in your journal. Web all the joyful moments in your life, that is, all the people and things that bring you joy. Write a poem that begins with the following question: Who are the bringers of joy? Answer this question using your list.

▪ Chapter 8 ▪

Writing a New World and Healing the Old One

Idealism is no longer a dream. It is a necessity.

—Lee Blessing

At the end of all our exploring
is to return to where we started and
know that place for the first time.

—T.S. Eliot

Now that we've had practice remembering, reflecting and intervening on our thoughts, we are freer to use that knowledge to reimagine ourselves and the world around us in a new way. This final chapter explores the power of looking beyond ourselves.

Life Is a Journey

Think of your life as a journey. Close your eyes and dream about the places you have been, the places you are going. Think of the things you have been through, the people or things you have yet to find.

1. Get a large blank piece of paper and draw a map of your journey from birth to the present moment. Use color pens, crayons or watercolors to represent different people who had influence in your life. For example, you could paint or smudge clouds to represent bad times or use dotted lines to represent unfulfilled dreams.

2. When you're done, look at your map. On a blank piece of paper list a series of moments when you felt you were close to life's Great Mystery, moments that connect with people who have guided

you, or places that had an other-worldly quality. If this doesn't make sense or seems too mystical, simply think of moments when you felt you made important decisions that gave direction to your life— moments when, like Robert Frost, you decided which path to take.

3. Pick three moments off your list and write about each of them. Draw pictures or cavewrites to go along with your writing.

Digging Deeper

What did you discover when you wrote about your moments? What have you learned in your life from these experiences? What is your personal definition of the Great Mystery? How do you define the higher power or the best part of you?

Writing Your Spiritual Autobiography

"I don't care what anybody says, life is a miracle." These were the last words my father spoke to me. It was a late August night and he and my mother were getting into their car. He was referring to their five-day-old granddaughter, Grace Shoshana, who lay asleep in her crib in the bedroom upstairs. Two weeks later my father was gone, but his words repeat in my mind whenever I look into my daughter's beautiful eyes. Life is a miracle. Life is a mystery. How can anyone, even the most scientific, rational of people think otherwise?

Apollo 14 astronaut Edgar Mitchell was an atheist until the moment he looked back at the earth from the surface of the moon. He wrote about that moment in his book *Psychic Exploration* (New York: Putnam, 1974).

> The first thing that came to mind as I looked at Earth was its incredible beauty. Even the spectacular photographs do not do it justice. It was a majestic sight, a splendid blue and white jewel suspended against a black sky. How peacefully, how harmoniously, how marvelously it seemed to fit into the evolutionary pattern by which the universe is maintained. In a peak experience, the presence of divinity became almost palpable and I knew that life in the universe was not just an accident based on random processes.

Just for a minute, close your eyes and imagine your own life is not a random series of events, but a process of transformation. What were you? What are you becoming? Where are you going? Where have you been? How does your life relate to the life of all human beings?

Throughout this book you have searched for meaning in your personal life and in the society in which you live. In this chapter we are searching for the larger meaning that connects all people, all societies. It requires imagination, faith and a desire to look beyond our own ego-bound selves to something greater. You have already taken the first step by exploring truth in your own life and your own society. You have pages of writing that prove this. Look back through them. Read them over and know the power you have to reimagine the world.

As I began writing my spiritual autobiography I revisited an experience I had the year I turned thirty.

It was 1986 and I had gone to Egypt to visit a friend who was teaching at the American University of Cairo. It was a watershed trip for me, the first time I had ever visited a third-world country.

When I arrived in Cairo that spring night I was immediately flooded with perceptions of raw sewage floating on side streets, policemen herding cars and donkeys with their big sticks and old rifles and beggars and peasant women selling tiny green lemons on the dusty sidewalk. I remember seeing a BMW pulling into a parking space where a peasant family sat eating their breakfast. Egypt was a strange and beautiful place, a place of extremes. On a side trip to Luxor to see the ruins of Carnac and the Valley of the Kings I did something I would later regret: I swam in the Nile. I didn't think anything of it at the time. But several days later back in Cairo I got very sick. It was a stomach flu like I'd never experienced before. That's when I picked up one of my travel books on Egypt. It said to never swim in the Nile. Sixty percent of the entire Egyptian population had bilharzia, an incurable illness contracted from a parasite that breeds prolifically in the Nile delta.

This wasn't enough for me. I made the mistake of consulting a medical textbook that happened to be in the apartment. Bilharzia was caused by a small liver fluke, a microscopic flatworm that swam right through the pores in your skin. I read this particularly graphic passage from the book: "The worms perform their grizzly court-ship ritual in the portal vein of the liver and swim up-stream finally attaching themselves to the bladder walls where they lay their eggs." This was enough to convince me I was seriously ill (even though bilharzia is not a ter-minal illness). I could feel the worms twisting and turn-ing in ecstasy as I lay there in bed. I knew I was dying.

Two weeks later I traveled to Northern Israel. I was convinced I still had the disease and was terminally ill. I made it to the town of Safed, a beautiful little hamlet overlooking the Sea of Galilee. I found a cheap hotel and was shown to my room by an old woman who walked with a limp. It was a small room with a big bed and a toilet. When we entered and she swung open the shut-tered windows over the bed, I saw the most beautiful view I had ever seen, a panorama of rolling hills and olive trees cascading down to the Sea of Galilee. It was like a full-color woodcut taken out of an old Bible. I thought to myself, this is the most beautiful place on earth. Then I thought of Moses gazing down at the promised land he would not be allowed to enter. My next thought was: *Like Moses, I have seen the promised land. I'm going to die here, tonight.*

Well, I didn't die there, but something happened as I lay there tossing and turning all night, thinking how utterly worthless my life had been; how all my strivings seemed so vain. You see my disease, the one I thought I had, was sort of a metaphor for the spiritual decay in my life. Even though I wasn't sick, I experienced the totality of my death. I grieved, not at the prospect of dying, but at the life I was living. I could feel the emptiness in my life and developed a strange hunger for something more. I realized that I was not aimlessly wandering for my religious roots. I was searching. I was searching for proof that there was more to life than what I had settled for. I was searching for a larger purpose. My life since this moment has reflected that search.

This was an important stop on my spiritual journey. Read over your own moments and pick one to explore further. Try one of these triggers.

Triggers

- Cavewrite one of the experiences you wrote about earlier.
- Answer this question in writing, painting, drawing, etc.: "What would it feel like to be taken care of?"
- Draw the stem of a flower, growing out of the earth. Imagine this flower is you. Where are you in the growth cycle? Are you budding, blossoming, fading or in full bloom? Complete your drawing. Then draw another flower of where you want to be. Get out your crayons and color your flower.
- On index cards write the major events of your life. A major event can be a marriage, graduation, etc., or a private moment when you discovered something. Now, on a large piece of paper, draw steps going up and steps going down. High steps represent life goals, low steps are setbacks. Place your cards on the right steps for their impact on your life. Write about what you discover in this map.
- Write a short poem about the unknowable. Draw a picture to go with it.
- Do a story wheel of your spiritual stories (see Chap. 6). What similar questions come up? Try freewriting an answer to one.
- Invite friends to your house to tell stories about their own spiritual journey. Don't let the S-word get in the way. Explain that this is about more than just religion. This is about how you personally developed or have not developed a belief in God, a soul, . . . the Great Mystery of the universe. Do a story circle with each person telling about their spiritual journey. While each person reveals a journey, the others write questions on scraps of paper. When each person has told a story, go back and read the questions. Pick the most interesting and turn them into leads. Pick a compelling lead and start writing.
- Write *God* in the middle of a page in your journal and web chart. Follow an interesting strand with a ten-minute freewrite.
- Draw a picture of three closed doors. Give them names to represent doors you have closed in your life. Now find a new piece

of paper and open one of those doors. Draw and write about what you see.

• Write a fictional story about a character who leaves home to go on a spiritual journey.

• Write a children's story about a character who discovers there is more to life than the material world.

• Get a big blank piece of paper. Write the year you were born on the left side and the present year on the right side. Close your eyes and let your hand draw a line across the page. Pretend that line is your spiritual journey. Let your hand describe its wanderings up and down and around as you think about events in your life. When you're done, open your eyes and take your spiritual EKG and write about each section of it. Share it with a group if you can.

• Pretend you have just died and are in the much-talked-about life review stage of death. List all the moments that flash through your mind. Which moments do you regret? Which do you cherish?

Cavewriting Your Cosmology

Life is a restaurant described by two elderly women patrons. One says, "The food is terrible." The other, "And such small portions."

—Woody Allen

All things are connected. You must teach your children that the ground beneath their feet is the ashes of our grandfathers.

— Chief Seattle

As we begin to explore a world larger than ourselves it's time to play with ways of defining how we see that larger world. A cosmology is a view of the universe. In ancient days, philosophers conceived and drew the universe according to their ideas about it. For example, the pre-Socratic philosopher Thales imagined the world as a large cylinder floating in an ocean of water. Ancient Babylonians viewed the world as mud that God formed into people.

Begin your cosmology by answering some of these questions. Don't be afraid if your ideas seem silly or crazy. Give your imagination some slack.

What is life made out of?

Where do we go when we die?

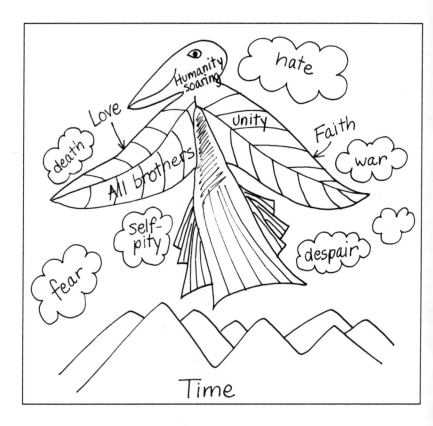

Where do ideas come from?
What keeps us alive?
If the world were an animal what would it be like?
If it were a vegetable what would it be like?
If it were a _____ what would it be like?

Now draw a picture of one or more of your answers. Embellish it with details and color. Call it your cosmology. Mine is shown above.

Digging Deeper

What is the dominant image in your cosmology? What does it say about you as a person? What can you add to your cosmology to embellish it?

A Matter of Faith

Bill Moyers, in a TV interview, asked Noam Chomsky, "What allows you to believe that humanity is essentially good? Couldn't you also assume that the opposite is true? How can you prove your assumptions?" Chomsky thought for a second, then replied matter of factly, "These are matters of faith and cannot be proven."

Chomsky's words have stuck with me because they seem a very sensible way of interpreting the world. They point to the failure of science to enlighten humanity. All things cannot be proven. Some things are "matters of faith." Firewalkers do not consult scientific evidence before walking over the coals. Faith motivates them.

In my cosmology faith is a large bird. One wing is the physical, the other the soul. We need both wings to fly.

What does your cosmology tell you about the world?

Triggers

• Try writing a cosmology of another planet where people are in some ways better or worse than earthlings.

• Write a poem describing your cosmology.

• Make a list of questions you always wondered about. Explain one of them with a made-up myth.

• Imagine a world in which men and women are truly equal without one gender dominating the other. Describe a TV commercial from that world. (Keep in mind that many commercials use women's bodies to sell products.)

• Write a letter to God about a problem you have. Then, imagine yourself as God and write a reply. What do you learn when you compare the two letters?

Imagining the Dream

Know ye not why We created you all from the same dust? That no one should exalt himself over the other. Ponder at all times in your hearts how ye were created.

—Bahá'u'lláh

What is it that stops us from imagining a newer, better world? One thing is the walls of hatred and distrust which have been passed down from one generation to the next. This next exercise examines the source of prejudice.

1. Write a detailed account of a time you were a victim of prejudice of any kind.

2. Now write a letter to the person who treated you with prejudice. Explain to the person their error. Try to write your response without anger. (It may take a draft or two to accomplish this.)

3. Read your letter. Feel the power of the truth in your words. Know that your truth is the same as everybody else's.

4. Now, pretend you are the other person and have just received the letter. Write back a letter of apology explaining the source of this unacceptable behavior.

Digging Deeper

What was it like to write your letter? What did you find out? What did you find out about prejudice when you became the other person and explained your story?

Revising Racism

Let your thoughts dwell on your own spiritual development, and close your eyes to the deficiencies of other souls.

— 'Abdu'l-Bahá

"I don't want your dumb Jew calender," Michael Waterman said to me that morning in second grade. "I threw it out!" We were on the playground lining up to go into the classroom. I remember how he quickly turned away when he said it and spit on the asphalt. I stood there frozen in my steps as he walked away, trailed by his other friends. I can still remember the feeling. It was more bewilderment than outrage. How could anyone be blind enough to assume they were better than you simply because they looked different or were from a different religion? Then came the fear, fear that there was something that I couldn't change. But even more than bewilderment and fear, it was just plain confusion. Why would a person hate another simply because they were supposed to?

Prejudice can be seen as a fundamental failure of imagination, an inability to imagine oneself as another. I'm writing this book in the wake of the South Central Los Angeles riots. The newspapers and television media have been full of stories as to why these events took place. The ability to see the connection between us, not the distance, is a skill which will all but eliminate racism and other forms of prejudice. In essence, it is the ability to see a larger context, to stand back and realize, in the words of Rodney King, "Can't we all live together?"

Look at your two letters from the last exercise. Notice how writing each one required laying aside blame and learning to trust. Racism and other forms of prejudice will disappear the more we learn to acknowledge but look beyond the walls of the past. Only then will we be able to answer Rodney King's question: "Yes, we *can* all live together."

Triggers

• Make up a racial stereotype for an imaginary race. They can be Martians or some other group. Now pretend to be a racist person defiling these creatures in a short speech. Note the utter absurdity of racism.

• Cavewrite a portrait of racial prejudice. Next cavewrite a portrait of racial unity. Hang both cavewrites on a wall and write about them.

• Pretend you are (if you are not) a member of a minority group. Imagine a moment when you encountered prejudice. Write about it in a letter to God. If you're from a minority group or have encountered prejudice of any kind, freewrite for ten minutes about this experience. Stop, read what you've written. Now write for another ten minutes pretending you are the person who put you down.

• Begin with the following words and write for ten minutes: "I have a dream. . . ."

• Make a list of things people can do to fight racism and prejudice in their life.

The Grand Illusion

The earth is but one country and mankind its citizens.
—*Bahá'u'lláh*

Close your eyes and imagine a new world—a better world. This is not a dream but a vision. You will not wake up from this vision because you can control it and work toward it. Nothing will stop you — not the chains of the past, the expectations and false hopes that have scarred us; not the ugly failures, such as wars, that have short-circuited civilizations and impeded the spiritual progress of individuals for centuries. We've looked at history. Now it's time to imagine a future worth projecting ourselves into. Begin with a list, or draw a large circle on a blank piece of paper and fill it with words and ideas. When you are ready, freewrite for ten minutes about this new world.

Digging Deeper

Does your new world feel attainable or does it feel like pie in the sky? What evidence can you cite in this world to help prove your new world already exists in an embryonic form? What can you find in today's newspaper that supports your vision?

Crisis in the Kremlin

No one was more surprised when the attempted coup de'etat in the Soviet Union failed than a certain California video company that was just about to release a new video game called "Crisis in the Kremlin." The game assumed that the player was Mikhail Gorbachev and the goal was to liberalize the old system as much as possible before the military intervened and toppled your government with a coup. Needless to say, the game was recalled after the failed coup and rewritten to include a new scenario. One wonders if the game has been revised several times since. The world today is changing much faster than our perceptions about it.

The founders of communism seemed to grasp the importance of an ever-evolving society. According to Engels, "Those who refuse to remember the past are doomed to relive it." Many rejoiced at the failure of the coup but many Americans, including myself, found it difficult to believe. After all, we had seen what happened in China at Tienanmen Square and hundreds of other similar situations. Surely the same thing was destined to happen here. If we only look backward for the truth, we will find the future mirroring only our past, a gruesome prospect for twentieth-century humanity to contemplate.

Our survival and the future happiness of our grandchildren depends on our ability to envision a new world, and to live in that world. Throughout this book you have personally begun the process of examining where you came from and reimagining your life in a new context. Think about it. This is precisely the same skill our entire species must learn if we are going to learn from our mistakes and forge ahead creatively into the next century.

Look at your vision of the world. Know that it is attainable. History only limits those who refuse to examine it, and who, through this failure of spirit, are afraid to imagine.

Triggers

• Write a letter to your great-great-great-grandchild. Explain the world you live in to them. Then write a reply from your great-great-great-grandchild explaining how life has changed since.

• Pretend you can go on vacation back into your past. You can visit your former self and see the context in which this self lived. Send a postcard back to your current self explaining anything you've seen on your journey.

• Write a pledge of allegiance for your new world.

• Write a poem with two repeating last lines in alternate stanzas: a new world, a better world.

• Make lists of details about your new world. Then write a brief description of one morning.

• Write the world *Unity* in the middle of a blank page. Web the word to tell about all aspects of unity in the new world.

The New You

Find a full-length mirror if you can. Stand in front of it. Look at the story of your life in your face, your eyes and the other parts of your body. Think of all the writing you have done in your journal and all the stories yet to be told. See the pain, the joy, the fear, the sadness, the awe of your life on this planet. Look closely into your eyes and know that you are here for a reason. Write a poem about yourself. Call it "Song of Myself" or "Ode to Me." You may want to begin by looking back through your journal and celebrating all the different parts of yourself you have unearthed using this book. Or maybe you want to cavewrite masks of yourself or dive right into freewriting.

Make it a poem that affirms something you have learned through reading this book or doing the writing. Let your poem be honest and direct. Let it speak from inside you like an honest voice. Don't worry if it's not perfect. Don't think too much. Just let the words spill out in whatever fashion they want to.

Draw a picture to go with the poem if the spirit moves you. Send it to a friend. Send it to my publisher so I can see it.

Digging Deeper

What does your poem tell you about your journey? What does it tell you about where you've been? What can you do? Here's what I wrote to me.

Ode to a Soul
I can see you
in there
I can see you
hiding in cracks
between pages
the air
between thoughts
You whisper to me
soft old songs
without melodies
like wind through leaves
I can see you
without shape or color
without smell or touch
I can see you
a bright shadow
in the dark
waiting in silence
a moment
pressed in black glass
veins growing memories
without breath or sadness
I can see you
the weight of years
gone
hope without pain

light chasing silence
and fear
to a world
without windows
or even
an eye
to look through them.

Triggers

- Write an ode to your son or daughter.
- Write an ode to one or both of your parents.
- Freewrite for ten minutes beginning with the words: "I'm glad I'm me because . . ."
- Make a chant poem with a repeating line that affirms something positive in your life. For example:

    Joyful day
    light in the morning
    joyful day
    new thoughts about old dreams
    joyful day
    I remember an old friend
    is coming
    joyful day . . .

- Write your own eulogy. Make it funny if you can. Reflect on the beauty of your life and your gratitude for the friendship of the mourners. Describe the process of living from your new perspective.
- Brainstorm a list for ten minutes following these four words: "I am grateful for. . . ." Let your list grow long and include people, places, things. Store a draft of your list. Staple it to your will and ask that it be read at your funeral.
- Make a list of good things you can do for yourself. Do one.

Come With Me

The last dream about my father began in a dark concert hall. The largest concert hall I had ever seen in my life. There were musical ensembles from all over the world and they were playing their own unique ethnic music all at the same time, but there was no confusion. You could hear all the music at once. I was there with my father, my old, about-to-die father. We were moving around listening to all the music. I turned to him, to see what he thought of the strange wonderful diverse sounds we were hearing. When I looked at him I noticed a strange, slightly catatonic look on his face. Then I saw him take something shiny from his pocket with his right hand. It was a harmonica and he was going to play it. I thought to myself, "This is embarrassing. My father doesn't play the harmonica. He is going to make a fool of himself." It seemed like a long time but it was probably only a few seconds, and finally the harmonica reached his lips. I watched him blow into the harmonica and in that moment the most amazing thing happened. The dark hall was suddenly full of bright light and all the musicians from all over the world who had been playing their instruments, stopped and cheered for my father at the top of their lungs. The sound is deafening. I look over at my father. He takes the harmonica away from his lips. The tears of joy roll down his cheeks. I wake up.

I have told many people this dream and have been asked many questions. Some think it is about my sense of reconciliation with my father. I am ashamed of him and awed by the universal music. Then the universal music stops and they cheer my father's humble efforts. My father's modest song is applauded by the concourse on high as though he were a great musician, a Horowitz in heaven.

I think this dream is about recognizing that all the unexpressed grief that weighed down my father's soul in this life will be expressed in the next world. I don't have to worry about him.

It left me feeling calm and totally at rest about my father's passing. I know that he is accepted where he is and that I don't have to worry about him anymore. I also know that though he is gone I can still learn from him and love him as much as I did when he was alive.

I hope that helped by these pages, you have begun the process of expressing your soul—however humble the effort. If I, in even the most modest way, have begun to help you begin this process, I am grateful.

I don't really know how to end this book. It seems to contradict the nature of what we've been doing to wrap up this discussion of writing, healing and self-discovery. A goal of this book has been to unlock your imagination from the past and allow you the freedom to explore your future. You have remembered, you have reframed and you have practiced reexperiencing and reimagining the world through new, clearer eyes. So maybe the best way to end this book is for us to begin another. Try this. Write a short poem beginning with the words: "Come with me. . . ."

Take your reader to wherever your heart desires. Know, like fourth-grader Susan Hall, that there are places inside you have only begun to imagine:

Come With Me
Come with me
to my favorite place
Come with me
to where secrets begin
Come with me
down
dark
hallways
to a place
never seen before
Come with me
to a new place
Come with me
to the end of the hallway
to a garden
only mine.

Body Mapping

Find a friend, a life-size sheet of paper and a magic marker. Lay down on the paper and have your friend trace your outline, the same way they do it for murdered people in movies. This is your body map. You can use it to stand back from the body you live in. Try writing memories from different parts of your body. Hang your body map on a wall near your writing desk. When you remember a bodily memory write it on the map. Try giving a voice to the parts of your body.

Brainstorming

Make a quick list of memories, ideas, details, questions or anything. Don't be critical. Let all your thoughts get to the paper. The power of brainstorming is that you give yourself permission to write everything down on the paper.

Cavewriting

As a cross between doodling and brainstorming, cavewriting is a technique to get you playing with thoughts on paper with more than words. Begin by making a sketch of something you are writing about. Next add words to the paper. Let your words and drawing reflect your emotions like an expressive cartoon. Try to get all your feelings and ideas down on the paper.

Chant

This is a poem with a repeating line as a chorus. The line can repeat as often as you want it to. Try writing a chorus that explores early memories, voices from the past, phrases, slogans, hopes, dreams. For example: Go away
I'm coming closer
Go away
don't take a step
Go away

you don't know me
Go away
why should I stay
OK
Go away.

Core Moments

This is a moment in your life when something important happened, something you will always remember. Try exploding a core moment and see what you remember.

Core Story

A core story is an essential story that replays itself over and over again in your life with different characters and different settings. We find our core stories by learning to stand back and see the patterns in the stories we tell over the years. Finding our core stories can help us to get a handle on the central questions of our lives and begin to answer them.

Exploding Moments

We explode a moment by returning to a short but important moment in our lives and expanding it over several pages, adding as much detail as we can to make the moment last. Think of yourself as writing in slow motion. Remember that writers have a great advantage over any camera because they can include smells, thoughts and feelings along with what they see.

Express Letters

An express letter is simply a letter that expresses what is in your heart. Try writing one to someone you have always wanted to tell your feelings to.

Firewriting

This technique can be used to make wild comparisons that may or may not lead to a greater understanding of a given situation. You begin by thinking of a subject you wish to explore. Then you start writing, all the time thinking of ways to connect what you write to something else to make a spark—a connection. Don't plan your sparks, let them occur in the flurry of free association. For example:

I am looking at the blue sky, it's the color of faded
jeans, the Caspian Sea. Why is the sky blue? Who painted
it blue? Blue is the color of the sky and sadness. Why is
sadness blue? The earth turns to the left, spinning blue
jean oceans . . .

Freewriting

Write faster than you can think. That's the one rule of freewriting. Pick a block of time, say seven minutes. Sit down with your pen
and paper and write without stopping for that length of time. Don't
screen out thoughts or erase anything. If you get stuck just write
down your thoughts and wait for the next idea.

Hand Mapping

Hand mapping is a technique for discovering ideas. Trace your
hand onto a piece of blank paper. Write a feeling or aspect of your
personality inside each finger. Draw lines from each finger and connect them with places, people and events. If you have children trace
their hands onto your hand map. Write down childhood needs for
all of your children's fingers. Think of your own childhood and
compare which needs got met for you with what you are providing
them. Let your thoughts trigger memories. Write them down on
the chart.

Leads

A lead is a journalistic term for the first line or two of a piece of
writing. A strong lead pulls both the writer and the reader in. Practice writing leads that make you want to write more. Try growing
leads from questions by simply answering the question. For example: Why didn't I do anything? Lead: I don't know why I just sat
there when everyone else was screaming.

Leap Essays/Poems

A leap essay is a when the writer makes analogies between disparate things in order to make a point. Begin by making a list of
ideas and branch off with metaphors and analogies when possible.
Compare things. Leap from one topic to another. Then look for the
connections.

Lyndy Loo Stories

If you are sick of writing in the first person, try writing in the third person about a character like yourself. This is a Lyndy Loo story. Give your character the problem you don't want to write about and see what happens.

Pain Poem

Poems can cut to the heart of a painful experience quicker than any other form I know. A pain poem is simply a poem about a painful experience. Here's one written by a fourth-grader. Think about how many more words the writer would have to use if this weren't a poem.

> **My burnt arm**
> Caps in a plastic bag
> hot day
> bang
> bye three layers of skin
> Clinic
> doctor
> bandage for a month
> arm better but have scar.

Potato

A potato is my term for the thing that makes a writer want to keep writing even when the lights go out. It is the thing the writer is trying to figure out.

Scenes

A scene is when two or more characters are talking to each other in a piece of writing. Scenes are usually composed of dialogue, thoughtshots and snapshots. For example:

Snapshot: He stood by the counter.

Dialogue: "Hi, Joe."

Thoughtshot: He hadn't see Joe in years. Joe hadn't changed.

Shifting Contexts

A context is the frame around any given experience. We shift contexts by creating a new frame. For example: A societal context might tell men they shouldn't cry, but an individual man can create a new context that says all men should cry. This new frame sheds light on the macho society that says men shouldn't cry. Shifting contexts helps us to reexamine the original context with new eyes. Try reframing yourself in a new context. Write about how it changes your perceptions of the original world (see page 79).

Shifting Points of View

Imagining ourselves as others helps us to see the big picture. We shift points of view by simply pretending we are the other person's point of view and looking at the world through their eyes. Try experimenting with unique points of view. Notice how a new point of view can change an old story.

Snapshots

A snapshot is a word picture of anything. As writers we possess magic cameras that can show us far more than light, color and shape. We can put smells in our pictures—thoughts too. Snapshot essays and poems are strings of word pictures held together by their association with each other.

Begin writing a snapshot as if you are holding a pair of binoculars at your subject. If you get stuck, ask yourself a question to turn the knob on the binoculars for a clearer picture. Try writing several snapshots of the same subject. Notice how sometimes the smallest detail can open up a new way of seeing the subject.

Splitting Personalities

Think of the different aspects of your personality and give them specific names—for example, the Jester, the Procrastinator and so on. Write a dialogue between them involving a decision you have to make. Try splitting the personalities of people you know.

Story Circle

Invite friends to your house and pass around a self-appointed talking stick. The stick gives you the right to talk. Everyone else listens. Note that this ritual is different than conversation because we don't interrupt each other. Notice and delight how one story sparks another.

Try focusing story circles on themes. Practice the joy of really listening to each other.

Story Cycle

Stories that get told and retold often change in meaning. This is what I call a story cycle. Discovering a story's movement through time is one way to understand the evolving meaning of that story. Try remembering how you told a particular story to different audiences at different times of your life.

Story Wheel

A story wheel is a device I created to track a story through time. (See page 126.)

Thoughtshots

A thoughtshot is a thinking report of a writer or a character. We write a thoughtshot by simply writing down the thoughts of an author or character. Thoughtshots can add reflection to a piece of writing. Practice writing down your thoughts in twenty-minute freewrites.

Web Chart or Webbing

Webbing is a way to take a helicopter ride above a subject. Begin by putting your subject in the middle of a blank page. Free associate words, ideas and memories off each strand. Relax and don't censor yourself. When one strand runs out go back to the nucleus and free associate another strand. Stand back and look for connections and areas of intrigue in your web. Freewrite about those areas and look for more areas of interest in your writing.

Further Reading

Here is a short annotated list of books which might aid you in further exploration.

Books That Model the Self-Discovery Process Through Writing

Anne Frank: The Diary of a Young Girl (New York: Random House, 1952)

Anne Frank's classic diary is still the best example I know of how writing can connect us with our emerging consciousness. Anne Frank was a twelve-year-old Jewish girl hiding from the Nazis in an Amsterdam warehouse with her family and several friends. Though she eventually died at Bergen Belsen concentration camp, her diaries are a living testament to the power of human spirit to have faith.

An Interrupted Life: The Diaries of Etty Hillesum (New York: Pantheon, 1983)

Etty Hillesum was a twenty-two-year-old Jewish art student when the Nazis invaded Holland. Like Anne Frank, her diaries chronicle the passion of a young idealistic mind coming face-to-face with the brute forces of history. Her bravery and faith are inspirational.

The Road From Corrain, Jill Ker Conway (New York: Alfred A. Knopf Inc., 1989)

This beautifully written memoir about Ms. Conway's childhood in the male-dominated world of the Australian outback and then, years later, eventually becoming president of Smith College, is a great example of a woman's rite of passage.

Selected Poems of Etheridge Knight (University of Cleveland Press, 1984)

Knight found poetry to be his salvation from prison life. His love of language and his rawness make his poems full of life.

Phillip Levine Selected Poems (New York: Atheneum, 1984)
Levine's poetry is both a journey of self-discovery and a chronicle of industrial and post-industrial American society.

*

Who Is the Widow's Muse?, Ruth Stone (Cambridge, MA: Yellow Moon Press, 1992)
Ruth Stone's husband, Walter, committed suicide many years ago. Each of these fifty-two poems explores a different dimension of the poet's core story—her grief and how she survived this event.

A Hole In the World, Richard Rhodes (Touchstone, 1990)
Rhodes's search to understand his abusive childhood illustrates the process of uncovering a long-buried core story.

Books on Faith and the Power of Stories
Man's Search for Meaning, Victor Frankel
Frankel's core story is about surviving Auschwitz and the ideas about humanity that grew out of that event. The first half of this book tells Frankel's story and how, despite all the odds, it was ultimately a positive experience. You will not easily forget Frankel's story and the example of faith he models.

The Call of Stories, Robert Coles (New York: Houghton Mifflin, 1989)
Harvard professor Robert Coles describes the power of literature to move people's lives.

Bahá'u'lláh and the New Era, J.E. Esslemont (Bahai Publishing Trust, 1950)
Bahá'u'lláh, prophet founder of the Bahai faith, lived one hundred years ago in Persia and preached about the unity of all religions, the equality of men and women, and the union of science and religion. This short book will inform you about this important man's life and give you insight into his world-embracing vision.

Peace on Earth: A Book of Prayers From Around the World, Bijou Le Tord (Bantam Doubleday Dell Publishing Group Inc., 1993)
A wonderful celebration of prayers and myths from around the

world, along with poetry and paintings. Bijou Le Tord's watercolors capture the mystery of faith and the spirit in all things.

Books on Using Writing to Heal

The Courage to Heal Workbook, Laura Davis (Harper Perennial, 1991)
This workbook is for both female and male victims of sexual abuse. Writing exercises focus on mining memory and learning to reclaim feelings numbed by time.

Pain and Possibility: Writing Your Way Through Personal Crisis, Gabrielle Garcia Rico (Jeremy Tarcher, 1992)
Rico's book uses right-brained techniques such as webbing to locate and work through personal crises.

Getting the Love You Want, Harville Hendrix (Henry Holt, 1988)
The exercises in this book are aimed at helping marriage partners understand each other's reality and learn to forge what Hendrix calls the "conscious marriage."

A Gift to Myself, Dr. Mark Hatfield (Health Communications, 1990)
Hatfield's book is full of exercises aimed at healing the child within.

Healing Racism in America: A Prescription for the Disease, Nathan Rutstein (Whitcomb Publishing, 1993)
If racism is a disease, Rutstein's book is a vaccination. Unlike most books on the subject, this one offers a practical blueprint for change.

Books on Learning to Love Writing and the Writer's Craft

Discovering the Writer Within, Bruce Ballenger and Barry Lane (Cincinnati: Writer's Digest Books, 1989)
Bruce Ballenger and I wrote this book to unlock the writer inside you that may still be intimidated by the ghost of a red-penciling teacher. If you have thirty minutes a day and a blank pad, this book will encourage you to find your inner voice as a writer.

If You Want to Write, Brenda Ueland (Greywolf Press, 1939)
Ueland's voice is direct and inspirational. Read it and get inspired.

Writing Down the Bones, Natalie Goldberg (Boston: Shambala, 1986)
Goldberg's book takes on the subject of writing to inspire the reader to put the book down, and pick up the pen.

Creating the Story: Guides for Fiction Writers, Rebecca Rule and Susan Wheeler (Portsmouth, NH: Heinemann Books, 1993)
This compelling and thorough guidebook is filled with fun exercises to help you understand and get excited about many different aspects of the fiction writer's craft.

The Curious Researcher, Bruce Ballenger (Boston: Allyn and Bacon, 1993)
Bruce Ballenger wrote this book to illustrate the joy of research writing. Told like a story, this book leads the reader through the different sides of research writing.

The Handbook of Poetic Forms, edited by Ron Padgett (New York: Teachers and Writers Collaborative, 1987)
This is a wonderful resource for anyone interested in exploring poetry. The book gives examples of many different forms of poetry and talks briefly about their origins.

After THE END: Teaching and Learning Creative Revision, Barry Lane (Portsmouth, NH: Heinemann, 1993)
I wrote this book to tune teachers and students in to the joy of revision. It explores ideas of craft and how to find your way back into a story you've written.

Shoptalk: Learning to Write With Writers, Donald M. Murray (Portsmouth, NH: Heinemann, 1989)
Donald Murray has collected thousands of quotes from professional writers to lend inspiration and insight into the process of writing.

Index

Other Books of Interest

General Writing Books
Discovering the Writer Within, by Bruce Ballenger & Barry Lane $18.95
Freeing Your Creativity, by Marshall Cook $17.95
Getting the Words Right: How to Rewrite, Edit and Revise, by Theodore A. Rees Cheney (paper) $12.95
How to Write a Book Proposal, by Michael Larsen (paper) $11.95
How to Write Fast While Writing Well, by David Fryxell $17.95
How to Write with the Skill of a Master and the Genius of a Child, by Marshall J. Cook $18.95
Knowing Where to Look: The Ultimate Guide to Research, by Lois Horowitz (paper) $19.95
Make Your Words Work, by Gary Provost $8.99
On Being a Writer, edited by Bill Strickland (paper) $16.95
Research & Writing: A Complete Guide and Handbook, by Shah Malmoud (paper) $18.95
Shift Your Writing Career into High Gear, by Gene Perret $16.95
The 30-Minute Writer: How to Write and Sell Short Pieces, by Connie Emerson $17.95
30 Steps to Becoming a Writer, by Scott Edelstein $16.95
The Writer's Digest Guide to Manuscript Formats, by Buchman & Groves $18.95
The Writer's Essential Desk Reference, edited by Glenda Neff $19.95
Write Tight: How to Keep Your Prose Sharp, Focused and Concise, by William Brohaugh $16.95

Fiction Writing
The Art & Craft of Novel Writing, by Oakley Hall $17.95
The Complete Guide to Writing Fiction, by Barnaby Conrad $18.95
Creating Characters: How to Build Story People, by Dwight V. Swain $16.95
Get That Novel Started! (And Keep Going 'Til You Finish), by Donna Levin $17.95
How to Write & Sell Your First Novel, by Collier & Leighton (paper) $13.95
Practical Tips for Writing Popular Fiction, by Robyn Carr $17.95
The 38 Most Common Fiction Writing Mistakes, by Jack M. Bickham $12.95
20 Master Plots (And How to Build Them), by Ronald B. Tobias $16.95
Writer's Digest Handbook of Novel Writing, $18.95

The Writing Business
The Complete Guide to Self-Publishing, by Tom & Marilyn Ross (paper) $18.95
How You Can Make $25,000 a Year Writing, by Nancy Edmonds Hanson (paper) $14.95
This Business of Writing, by Gregg Levoy $19.95